UNLOCKING THE HEART

UNLOCKING THE HEART

Writing for Mindfulness, Courage, and Self-Compassion

JAMES CREWS

FOREWORD BY MARK NEPO

MANDALA

SAN RAFAEL LOS ANGELES LONDON

For all my teachers,
past and present

Table of Contents

FOREWORD

James Crews is a clear and tender poet. He is in the lineage of those who believe that we all are poets when loved or worn into being authentic. Poets such as Walt Whitman, Rainer Maria Rilke, Pablo Neruda, William Stafford, Stanley Kunitz, Galway Kinnell, Jane Kenyon, Sharon Olds, and Naomi Shihab Nye. This is the poetry that sustains us because the life of expression is constantly healing. This opens everyone to a deeper practice than just arranging words on a page. This is the poetry that rises from the inner life to shape the outer life. This is the poetry that saves us each time we stumble and fall.

Ultimately, art that matters issues from the common well of our humanity, revealing our universal experience through our very personal experience, if we can be searingly honest in our giving and endlessly tender in our receiving. James does both. The poems alone in this collection are poignant, precise, and life-giving. But the commitment to our common journey has stirred James to go even further by adding a reflection and a writing prompt after each poem, as a way to encourage your own expression and growth.

And so, Unlocking the Heart is not a set of instructions but an offering of lyrical thresholds which, by their gentle truth, invite us into the wisdom of our own journey. I encourage you to take your time in reading and writing your way through this book. I encourage you further to bring what you find to friends and strangers alike. For we need to travel in the lineage of honest company, if we are to find each other. As James affirms in lines from his poems, "We are changed by the smallest gestures . . . [so] open your hand and trust whatever lands there."

With thanks to poets like James Crews, we can enter this journey to the heart of living, that is both timeless and immediate, and meet each other there.

—**Mark Nepo**

INTRODUCTION
What Brings You Alive

I began writing poems in the third grade when my teacher, Mrs. Brown, required us to memorize and recite a new poem every week. Though I was a shy and introverted kid, I somehow worked up the courage to approach her desk, and asked if I could write and recite my own poems to the class. Mrs. Brown's eyes lit up, and she clapped her hands as my face turned a deep shade of red. "Yes!" she said, drawing the curious glances of my classmates. I don't know what strange call led me to her desk that day, or what gave me the bravery to stand up in front of everyone at the end of the week and share the poem I had written, "An Ode to Summer." But I still remember friends coming up to me during lunch and recess, confessing how much they had enjoyed my poem, surprised that I could write like that. Seeing other people react to something I'd made myself out of nothing but my own thoughts and words planted a seed in me that would keep me writing in the years to come, in spite of the fears and doubts that so often accompany the process.

I strive to write poems that anyone can enter because I see writing as the ultimate healing practice. Some of us may not be experienced writers, but most of us can write, and have even tried our hand at poetry at some point. Like the late poet William Stafford, I believe we are all born poets, with the ability to see the world in fresh and exciting ways. Because we're often not encouraged to keep flexing this muscle, and because many of us have been discouraged at certain points in our lives, we forget that our imagination remains available to us, and is always making new connections. The pressure to find safety and financial stability can also make us turn from our dreams. Even as recently as a few years ago, I took an office job that simply wasn't right for me, believing I needed to be more practical and responsible. I gave up the time I usually spend delightedly scrawling in my notebook each morning to drive over an hour to a stuffy, lightless cubicle. Almost instantly, I began losing my hair, my skin broke out, and a depression descended that kept me in bed for a week. What saved me was poetry, realizing that I needed that time and space in my life to release all that was inside. If we want to be creative, self-compassionate, and mindful beings in this world, and I believe we all do, then we need the permission to choose what brings us alive over and over, knowing we deserve the deep joy of self-expression. But we don't need to quit our jobs or change our lives completely to do that. As I made more space for words to pass through me and onto the page, it became clear that it takes so little each day to keep the creative spark lit. I hope that some of the poems gathered here can become faithful companions on whatever journey you might face, helping to the light the way.

Poetry can be the gateway to any creativity. You might read one of the poems in this book and suddenly recover a memory you had no idea you still had. You might be inspired to paint, knit, or call a friend you haven't spoken to in years. Reading or writing a poem can help us step outside of daily life for a few shining moments and look at our world as an observer. We see once-familiar things and people with fresh eyes, finding new images and insights to carry with us. In one of the poems in this book, for example, I write about a summer afternoon spent with my husband, Brad, on the couch. Nothing really happens in the poem, but by taking down all the images that called to me—the peach waiting on the counter for the "kiss of the knife," the hairs on his arm gone golden from hours in the sun—I realized how grateful I felt for these few plain hours together when it was too hot to do much else.

Poetry invites us to meet every moment with vulnerability and a clear heart, but it's not always an easy or comfortable way to move through life. Maybe, like me, you have those days when simply opening the door and exposing yourself to other people feels painful, almost impossible. We are bound to feel overwhelmed at times by this noisy, demanding world of ours, yet my hope is that the poems, reflections, and writing prompts in *Unlocking the Heart* allow you to slow down and step out of worry and anxiety for at least a few minutes, able to take a deeper breath. You might read one entry a day as part of your morning routine, or keep the book on the bedstand at night to absorb before sleep.

My intention is that in reading these poems and reflections, many of which were written during the most challenging times of my life, you will see them as openings into your own experience and invitations to hold both the sorrows and joys at once. Because I trust that we all have access to the renewing powers of writing, I have included reflections and prompts throughout the book that you may use as part of your own journaling or spiritual practice. As you read these, feel free to let your mind run wild in its own directions, even beyond the prompts I provide, and don't worry about writing in a "right" or "wrong" way. This book is not just for poets or writers, but for anyone looking to lead a more coura-geous and present life. Let the images and scenes in these poems help guide you through the ordinary blessings and obstacles of each new day. Let them become friends when you find yourself confused about where to turn, or feel alone in your pain. Above all, let them point the way to the small things that bring you alive because, as the Reverend Howard Thurman once famously said, "What the world needs is people who have been brought alive." Your heart may feel broken, but we can make it a daily practice to love the world and ourselves, gently unlocking each of the closed doors inside us.

—James Crews

PART ONE

Poems for Courage and Vulnerability

What if joy, instead of refuge or relief from heartbreak, is what effloresces from us as we help each other carry our heartbreaks?

—Ross Gay

Kintsugi

Anyone who loves someone else
already has a broken heart.
It's the law: If you want that light
to flood your body, you must
expose the scars through which
it pours, for they are the source
of your beauty and strength.
Think of the Japanese who fill
the cracks in a ceramic bowl
with pure gold, not only flaunting
those so-called flaws, but also
making each one a priceless vein
through which light now moves.

It can seem as if we were shaped so tenderly
and carefully by some unseen hand, only to
be thrust into the kiln-like fires of life.

Losses, illness, and deep disappointment can harden us against life until we grow bitter and brittle, never wanting to let love in again. Yet it is a law that we must lead ourselves—or be led—into risk and discomfort to learn what we are capable of holding. We must pass through the fire before we can fulfill our destiny of acting as a vessel, allowing ourselves to be filled over and over by what the world offers, and giving it back as often as we can.

In my own life, each trip through the fire has left me both drained and somehow stronger, in spite of the countless scars that have also appeared. I have had to surrender to the process of being made into something new that is imperfect compared to the vision I once had for myself. I must admit that when my father died at the young age of 43, and when a longtime partner left me a few years later, I did not make it out of those fires fully intact. I was cracked down the middle several times, unable to hold anything or anyone properly for a long time after. Yet time also mends, and over the years, I have opened to the truth of our essential brokenness because I understand that we are whole and complete just as we are, no matter the so-called flaws. I know that, as my poet-friend Heather Swan has pointed out: "It is at the edge of damage that beauty is honed."

In fact, it was Heather who first explained to me the Japanese practice of *kintsugi*—filling the cracks in a ceramic bowl with gold, highlighting the supposed failures, while at the same time making the bowl stronger and more valuable. Since then, I have learned to tend my own damage in this way. Instead of covering up my scars, which never works, or pretending they don't exist, I show them to others who have earned my trust. I choose to see each one as beautiful and necessary, part of what has made me wiser and more compassionate, part of what allows me to keep loving in spite of it all.

INVITATION FOR WRITING & REFLECTION

Do you feel as if the fires you've had to pass through over the years have left you broken open, but somehow stronger? What scars have you chosen to keep hidden, and how might you highlight them now for yourself so they shine like priceless veins of gold in a mended bowl?

The Eyes of the Heart

If you keep your eyes open,
you will see the carpet of dandelions
spread across the greening yard,
and a grateful bee rolling in the petals
of each one. You will see the pollen
gathered in sacs on the back legs
of a bumblebee, but you must keep
the eyes of the heart open to feel
the need that drives the hovering body
from flower to flower. You must sense
with a wise heart the wild desire
of a dandelion's taproot to stay alive.
Even with its leaves and blooms
ripped away, still the root remains,
clinging to soil as you hold fast
to what feeds your heart too, refusing
to let go, though others beg you,
though they tug and tug.

Most of us know what it feels like *not* to see with the eyes of the heart.

Our lives often train us and tug us toward so-called rational choices that may take us away from what we truly love. And we too, feeling the pull of logic and thinking with our heads, may talk ourselves out of what feeds us, believing that life's true callings are duty and responsibility to others only. I know what it is like to live with the eyes of the heart shut tightly against the world, just going through the motions, dwelling on the surface of things, without the devotion that lets us look harder and feel into the lives around us. I remember working a demoralizing office job not long after graduate school, tucked inside my cubicle, doing good work that simply was not right for me. Every day I woke with a longing to stay at my desk and write, pouring my heart out onto the notebook page in front of me, watching rain caress the limbs of the maples outside my window. Yet instead of finding a way to listen to the deeper call of my creativity, I lost hope, lost heart, and turned off that part of myself to keep showing up at a job I could not stand, in a place that never felt like home.

Eventually, I felt my eyes pried open to the beauty of the world again. I began to "see small" once more, paying close enough attention for my life to speak to me, for my poetry to teach me how I needed to live. But I soon realized this would not be enough. For me to live more fully in the timeless flow of each day, I would need to see with the eyes of the heart that always guides us where we need to go. And so began a lifelong practice of immersing myself in the world at hand, in the people in my direct orbit, and in the living beings of nature all around me. We can see the details of dandelions, for instance, and even describe them quite beautifully, but we cross a necessary threshold when we feel our way into the heart of that flower we call a weed and notice the bumblebee with its pollen sacs on each leg. We awaken when we see the life at play in everything. This is not a practice we can master, but one that we must return to again and again, whenever we feel ourselves peeled away from what's essential to us, what fuels us. We can forget that we carry nature's resilience within us too, and that we are allowed to listen to the intuitive, heart-centered voice that leads us toward what we need, no matter what others might say. If you've found something that brings you to life, don't listen to those well-meaning people whose own hearts may be locked up and blocked from their truest joy. Listen to yourself and choose over and over to see with the eyes of your own heart, refusing to let go of what calls to you, what feels like home.

INVITATION FOR WRITING & REFLECTION

Write about all the specific things you see when you pay deeper attention and keep your eyes open to the small. Then write what you see with the eyes of the heart, what feels true to you about the world, even if you can't logically prove it. You might begin with the phrase, "If I keep my eyes open . . ." and see where that carries you.

The World Loves You Back

Even if no one ever touched you
with the tenderness you needed,
believe that the world's been
holding you in its arms since
the day you were born. You are
not an accident, or afterthought.
Let rain on the roof remind you.
Let sun on the skin, and the neon-
orange of the Mexican sunflower
at which a hummingbird pauses
to drink. There are so many ways
to hold and be held, and you
could spend your whole life
tallying them up, without ever
reaching the end of the list.

Most of us probably grew up without certain
things we needed—not enough tenderness or touch,
not enough encouragement or attention.

And yet, here we are, still able to feel moments of presence and joy, able to see the many ways we choose to hold and be held by the world. This poem expresses something that I have been trying to say for well over a decade, when these words first started stirring in me while on a solo writing retreat at the Oregon coast. When we can allow the very simple things around us to offer themselves to our attention, we gain brief access to qualities that can seem so fleeting, but are no less necessary—wonder and awe, courage and a useful vulnerability. Yet we gain a fuller presence in the world only by staying open to it, accepting the exposure that comes with letting ourselves be touched by this intimacy with everything and everyone around us. The sound of rain on the roof then becomes an ancient lullaby; the feel of sun on the skin turns into a blessing we happily accept. Perhaps our task while here is to spend our lives tallying up all the ways we feel held by this physical world and all of the things we love about it, so that it becomes more difficult to lose sight of our aliveness and the gift of one more day on Earth.

INVITATION FOR WRITING & REFLECTION

What are some of the ways the world reminds you that you too belong here? What specific things ground you in your life and offer you the courage and bravery to stay open, in spite of the ways you might have been harmed in the past?

Hermit Thrushes at Dusk

The long summer day's gone quiet at last
in the open-air cathedral of the woods,
yet still I hear the hermit thrushes unraveling
their complex calls, like someone running
a finger along the rim of a wineglass
over and over, out in the trees, their music
made more precious by the silence
surrounding it, more necessary by the worry
that encircled me all day, keeping me
from this world I love. I listen, freeing myself
from the tangled roots of a fear
that's not my own, and drink in those clear
liquid notes like a medicine, a message
I have craved my whole life without knowing:
Let go of all that you no longer need.
This is how you heal, using your body to sing.

When we are exhausted, perhaps from tending
the needs of others, one of the best gifts
we can offer ourselves is simple presence,
an opening of the senses.

We forget that mindfulness is available at all times, and when we attune our attention to the world again, we find ourselves more in touch with life, our bodies beginning to calm. If we've been going at a speed that feels unsustainable, against our own slower nature, then stillness will likely feel hard to embrace at first. We may have to ease ourselves into it, like slipping into the cooler water of a pool. This was certainly true for me on the summer day I describe here, when I finally sat down long enough to listen to the hermit thrushes calling to each other in the woods around my house at dusk. The song of these birds has become a kind of soundtrack for my summers in Vermont, yet this was a season of caregiving and overcommitment with work. I had strayed so far from the habits of self-care that taking even five minutes for myself before preparing dinner seemed like a radical act that made me jittery and restless. Luckily, I remembered—while hearing that music through the windows, watching sunlight fade through the trees—that if I sat through this discomfort, eventually I would reach the place of peace that waits on the other side of any agitation.

There is a kind of body-and-soul relief that falls over us when we take the time we need to heal from moving too fast through the world, from caring too much for others. As I remind myself over and over, it doesn't take much to come back to center. Often, it's deciding to sit and write that allows me to see why I've become so distracted in the first place. As soon as we feel the pull to pick up our devices, send one more email, finish one more task before the end of the day, maybe we can ask ourselves: What simple thing will give me pleasure right now and make me feel more alive? Stepping into what we have right here is the gateway to presence, joy, and creativity. That's when we begin to use our bodies to sing, healing from the rush and busyness that easily overtake us.

INVITATION FOR WRITING & REFLECTION

Even if you don't feel that you have the time, try to set aside just five minutes (or more) to listen to your world, to open your senses to what is around you. What do you notice? What helps you heal from the harmful speeds at which we so often move through life? You might start with the phrase, "This is how I heal . . ." and see what feels true for you.

After the Fire

Let me endure whatever fires must
pass through here, must scorch my skin.
And if I have to feel the heat, let me
also trust that like the lodgepole pine,
the fire will open the parts of me
that are still closed tight, releasing seeds
I've been clinging to, hoarding for years.
Let me thrive in this new clearing
made at the center of my life, seeing now
how the necessary flames melted away
my resistance, revealing all that once
lay hidden, asleep inside me.

Often, we end up writing what we ourselves most need to hear.

I began working on this poem one day when I struggled with extreme fatigue and burnout, feeling distraught by all the bad news and the continual fight for justice. The next day, on a long drive through the countryside, the poem came back to me from memory, and I began saying it over and over to myself almost like a mantra, needing to believe that we all come through our personal and collective fires with more resilience, feeling stronger and more aware of our gifts for having walked through the difficulties.

I also considered the many times that my own fires have brought me closer to who I am and my own authenticity, especially when I lost my mother recently. Her sudden death brought me again to the healing power of poetry and writing and helped remind me that what I do is not just a hobby or profession, but a profound spiritual practice to which I am devoted. The pain of sitting with her for that final week in the hospital, as dementia began to take over and she struggled to let go, released the seeds of my creativity and strength. While we will have to feel the pain and grief of whatever fires pass through our lives, we do not have to be defined by them. Sometimes, things must fall apart for something new and more lasting to emerge from the sudden clearing that is both loss and possibility.

INVITATION FOR WRITING & REFLECTION

Where do you find examples of resilience and strength in your own life? Can you remember a specific time when you came through a fire of your own stronger and perhaps more aware on the other side? You might begin with the words "Let me endure . . ." and let them guide you like a difficult incantation.

Trust

Though I may not feel it yet today,
I want to be as brave as the tiny
merganser duckling who, as soon as he
chips his way through the cracking egg,
must leap from the old woodpecker hole
high up in a tree where his mother chose
to hide her nest lined in feather- down.
I want to leave all safety behind,
and trust that the ground will hold me,
that my body was built for risks like this.
Even while falling through empty air,
let me believe I will bounce back,
still as resilient as that first moment
my unsteady feet touched the earth.

Merganser ducklings must make a leap out into the world within hours of first emerging from the shell.

When I learned this, I felt astounded by the level of resilience and courage expected of them so soon, with little time to adjust to their new reality. I also began to think about all the leaps we make in our own lives—first words, first steps, first day of school—and how they imprint on us, building strength little by little along the way. Every time we make something new or sit down to write, we are also taking a creative leap. But what if we approached such risks with trust placed alongside the fear and resistance that also accompany us? What if we could hold onto some of the innocent faith that seemed to arise for us effortlessly as children, trusting that the ground of our lives will hold us each time we step out into the "empty air" of uncertainty? We may not know what awaits us on the other side of creative risk, and we may not even know where a piece of writing will take us. But we can do our best to cultivate a sense of surprise, taking delight in the not-knowing, and what shows up when we follow our instincts and push ahead.

As someone who's struggled with lifelong anxiety, the idea of leaving behind all safety and trusting the ground to hold me whenever I take a risk is not exactly welcome or comforting. Yet perhaps that is the point; as author Neale Donald Walsch has said: "Life begins at the end of your comfort zone." This does not always mean doing dangerous things either, risking our lives by skydiving or swimming with sharks. It can feel dangerous to sit with someone who's just received a difficult diagnosis, or to accept the steady love of someone when all you've known in your life thus far is chaos and drama. It might feel like stepping off the edge of the earth to speak our heart and mind, to ask for what we need, to apply for a new job, or end a toxic friendship. What helps me the most in times of transition, when I'm about to make a leap that seems to threaten my whole being, is to remember: I've done hard things before. We may not always trust the outer world, but we can place faith in our own courage, in the strength we have built up over time. As we grow older, and if we keep trying to grow as human beings, the leaps will only keep coming. We just need to carry with us the image of those tiny, vulnerable ducklings tumbling from their hole high up in a tree, with no choice but to meet the ground beneath them with absolute trust.

INVITATION FOR WRITING & REFLECTION

Can you think of a leap of your own that you took recently? How did your own faith and resilience carry you and help ground you? You might begin with "I want to be as brave as . . ." and see what your own imagination fills in.

Human Being

The human part of us
wants and needs and breaks,
but the being part sees
beyond the body's aching
joints and joyful noises
to the open road ahead.
The gravel is covered
in a fine layer of snow
and ice with the white sun
shining through a tunnel
of pines like the unblinking
eye of the source.

The human part of us
knows that if we keep going
we will slip and slide
and fall down endlessly,
but the being part says
so what? and pushes us
onward toward the light,
since it knows there is
no way but to move
forward, step by step
in our heavy boots.

When we create anything, when we love wholeheartedly, when we reach out from our depths to help care for another, the human part of us speaks to the being part.

We become more aligned with our spiritual side. Creation allows us to see the Source or God revealed like a sudden sun glimpsed through a tunnel of pines on a snowy day. And uniting these halves of our whole self is one of our purposes while here on Earth. We are here to find joy and transcendence in making or fixing or tinkering—without the expectation of success or money or status, though these may come at certain times. Even when we keep this deeper intention at heart, however, the human part of us can easily slip into fear of judgment or rejection by others. This is still one of my most potent anxieties: that I will reveal myself completely through my poetry and writing and will then be ridiculed and laughed at by the people I respect the most.

Yet each instance I sit down to write or try anything for the first time, I let the being part of me take the reins and lead me forward. When I can keep a clear channel open, giving myself the space I need for play, and gently remembering that there can be no attachments to outcome when it comes to art, my whole being seems to rejoice with the permission simply to *be*. And when I start fearing again the unavoidable pitfalls of so-called failure, the being part says, "So what?" and reminds me that this path was never about comfort or safety. Then I keep trudging on with the faith that whatever we make deeply matters, that all creation connects us back to the Creator and instantly brings us closer to each other as well. We can trust in this truth, even while wearing the heavy boots of self-doubt and fear, pushing ourselves onward step by slow step, always following the light.

INVITATION FOR WRITING & REFLECTION

Can you recall a time when you felt the being part of you speaking to the human part, when you felt more aligned and whole? Describe how it felt on a physical level to lose yourself in some creative task or chore that you deeply enjoy. How might you find creativity in any act, no matter how mundane it seems, and let it transform you?

Prayer to Be Changed

I ask for just the slightest shift
in my thinking, the kindest sifting
of my busy mind so only wonder
and peace are left behind. So that
as I walk in sleet on this spring morning
I can see even these muddy ruts
made by careless trucks on the forest trail
as harbors of miracle, knowing they will
fill with enough snowmelt and rain
for tadpoles to swim in come summer,
until that sunlit instant when they feel
the flexing of legs in the water beneath them,
and leap out onto the ground, their bodies
having decided, by pure instinct alone,
to be soft and alive in this world.

We have so little control or power over anything outside of ourselves.

Yet what we *can* control is how we see and frame our experiences. Thus, the most potent form of prayer is the kind by which we ask our higher power, however we conceive of them, to change our minds, to help us view things in a new way. I wrote this poem on a gray Easter morning, with sleet spitting at every window. As I took my daily walk, everything seemed a source of annoyance, especially the deep and damaging ruts left by pickup trucks on the forest trail near our house. Though I felt no hope for an improvement in my mood, as I walked in mud and slush, searching for some sign of rebirth in the wakening ground, I asked for the slightest shift in my thinking so I might salvage at least part of that Sunday.

By the time I came inside and sat down with a cup of tea, some new words were stirring inside me. I took out my notebook and pen, and decided to listen, copy down whatever I heard. In giving shape to what I was feeling, I found that I was indeed slowly changed. As Mark Nepo has written: "The sudden view at the end of every poem is the unexpected teacher, the reward for following our feelings into the open." I never feel worse after journaling or writing down my experience, getting the dark thoughts out of my head and onto the page, creating something new, whether out of joy or pain. As I wrote, I remembered that those muddy ruts, which I'd been so frustrated by, often become harbors of miracle and wonder, hosting tadpoles in late spring as they fill with snowmelt and rain.

Sometimes writing becomes a kind of prayer in and of itself, and whether we know it or not, our minds and bodies are slowly altered by the attentive act of letting words flow through us. As we practice saying "yes" more often to what arises, soon the decision to embrace each new moment as fresh and filled with possibility becomes as automatic as the flexing of a frog's new legs, and we feel we can take the leap into a new way of seeing our world.

INVITATION FOR WRITING & REFLECTION

The next time you feel the heaviness of anxiety or despair pressing, try asking for even the slightest shift in your thinking. You might ask out loud, or do so in writing. Once your question's released, see what calls to your attention. Can you find some of your own harbors of miracle that give you the courage to be both "soft and alive in this world?"

Monarch

The butterfly does not break free triumphant.
Once it claws through the chrysalis,
it stands there shivering, new wings aching
as they slowly fill with blood. It must keep
its tiny eyes shut tight at first against
the brightness and shimmer of a world
it has never seen before—not like this.
It must listen until the soul's voice whispers:
The flowers are waiting. Leave the skin
of the old life far behind. Open your eyes
and give in to the blue air that will carry you
everywhere you need to go.

If you've ever watched a butterfly claw its way out of the chrysalis, you know that such emergence is not a gentle process.

Once it has finally struggled out of the skin that protected it for months, the butterfly must then consume it for strength and stand there while its new wings fill with blood. In the space of those few moments on a branch, it is never more vulnerable or exposed to threats from the natural world. A predator could easily swoop in and end this new life before it even begins.

So it is with us. We create protective skins around ourselves, and even if they begin to constrict and stifle, even if the darkness becomes unbearable, still we resist leaving because the tight spaces have become familiar and comfortable. It can be difficult to convince ourselves to surrender the safety of our old skin, too, if we know that complete exposure and uncertainty await us on the other side of this work of becoming.

Yet risk is the only way we become who and what we were meant to be. And there always comes a moment when the pain of staying small becomes greater than the pain of true growth, as the soul whispers of a new life waiting beyond the known. We might ache for the old ways of life just as the butterfly, as it flaps new wings for the first time, must wonder why it needed to go through such painful changes in the first place. As we grow used to the feeling of being free, however, of having the space of the entire world at our disposal, instead of just the cramped rooms of the mind, we might then wonder why we waited so long to break through and seek the light of day. We might ask ourselves: Why have I been crawling when I could have been flying the whole time?

INVITATION FOR WRITING & REFLECTION

What protective skins have you created for yourself over the years? Try to be as specific as possible when you describe the places, people, and situations that might have kept you small. Did your chrysalis feel comfortable and safe, and was there a moment when it stopped feeling that way, when you began to hear the whispers of some new life calling to you from deep inside yourself?

Choosing the Light

We think of wildflowers as fragile,
amazed at the way they shoot through
layers of soil and plowed-up gravel
on the raw cusp of spring each year,
sensing some new heat and invitation
in the sun, often long before we do.
But as I kneel beside the first tiny
yellow coltsfoot to appear in the yard,
in ground I'd think too rocky and cold
for any living thing, I see they are
not delicate. I notice the segmented
stems that must have guarded each bud
as they pushed upward like spears
to pierce the warmer air. Relentless
as the urge that also blooms in us
sometimes—to find the one thing
that brings us alive, and open ourselves
fully to it, never giving up and saying
to the world: Do to me what you must.
Knowing it will have been worth it
to spend even just one day, a single hour,
exposed to the light we chose.

I don't know why it always feels like such a gift to see the first signs of spring—wildflowers like coltsfoot and snowdrops shooting up, the suddenly warmer sun that has clearly grown in power since early winter.

But spring often arrives for me like an awakening from a long sleep, like a true new year. In this poem, I became fascinated with the way we think of wildflowers, also called "ephemerals" for how quickly they fade, as somehow fragile or delicate. In reality, it takes great resilience and strength to keep coming back year after year, to push through the human-made layers of gravel spread on the roads during winter. This same call to rise toward the light also visits us at times, "to find the one thing that brings us alive" in a given moment, even if that shifts and changes over time. We can grow overly obsessed with finding our one calling in the world, when a better question we might ask ourselves is this: What calls to me right now, in this moment? What do I enjoy doing that I would keep doing no matter what? It can be uncomfortable to answer the call, to reveal ourselves vulnerably after a difficult season, but I know that, for me, it has always been worth it to live even briefly in the warmth and authenticity of the light I chose, following my own deepest desires to share my gifts with the world.

This has certainly been true of my journey as a poet. I have had to learn over the years how to keep moving through each new blockage, how to continue revealing myself wholeheartedly in my writing, especially when the seductive desire to hide returned again and again. When I was young, I would tape poems I loved to my bedroom walls, never dreaming that I would publish my own books someday, or that I would gather poems I loved into anthologies that other people would read and appreciate. I was only responding to what called to me, and eventually started filling notebooks with poems of my own. Only in the past few years have I adopted a "mind of abundance" when it comes to my creativity. I felt afraid for so long of opening and blooming in a world that would no doubt judge and criticize me. I didn't think I would be able to handle the exposure, and often worried I was too weak to weather the harshness of others when it came to my art. What I have found, however, is that the more I share, offering my work as freely as I can to the world, the more I am called back to the page, back to the vulnerability of opening myself to whatever wants to move through me.

INVITATION FOR WRITING & REFLECTION

Describe a time when you showed up vulnerably in the world, or shared your creativity with someone else. Did you feel it was worth it to reveal your truest self? What other examples of such open-hearted presence can you find around you, perhaps in the natural world?

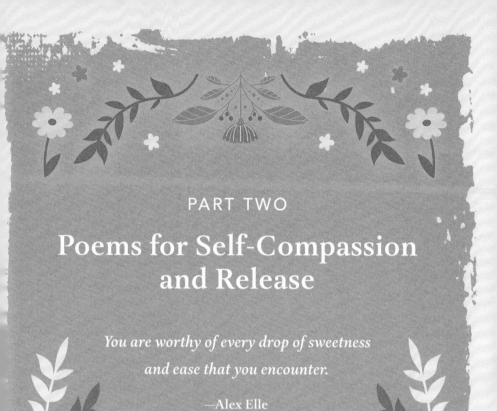

PART TWO

Poems for Self-Compassion and Release

You are worthy of every drop of sweetness
and ease that you encounter.

—Alex Elle

After Burnout

You finally decide to do no more
than is necessary, relishing each new
gulp of air drawn into your lungs,
when out of the flavorless mush
of days, even weeks without sun,
it happens again: life calls you back.
With a hint of chocolate in the cup
of coffee taken alone at the table,
or the needles of coneflower seeds
sticking to your fingertips as you
spread them around in autumn earth.
How all living things want to go on,
attaching themselves to whatever body
or breath of wind will carry them home.
Now stop in the driveway and listen
as amber-gold leaves, one by one,
break off with a simple snap of stem
from branch, that sound just shy
of silence saying to you: it's time
to release all the relentless reaching
for the light. Rest is not death,

Burnout and other forms of deep stress cut us off from our natural connection to the outer world, with its wisdom and many healing properties.

I can still remember well the recent autumn that I describe in this poem, when all the maple leaves in our yard turned the most striking shade of amber-gold. But I was hardly there to see it, to feel the changes happening. I had spent so long taking care of my husband and mother, both of whom had fallen ill several times, and I had worked too much, pushing myself so hard, until each new day felt flavorless and gray. In the midst of it all, I lost the capacity to find joy in the smaller moments that have always spoken to me.

I began to feel relief, if not a full recovery, when I allowed myself the space of several days without interaction, work, or social media. Having finally named the burnout I was experiencing, I soon realized I had become an input addict, taking in and taking in—often the problems or struggles of others—without stopping to release some of that absorbed pain. As Oprah Winfrey has said: "You can't keep giving from an empty cup." And my cup was drained. I refilled it with solitude and stillness, reading and taking walks in the garden and woods around our house. Just those few instants of noticing the shriveled-up and blackened coneflowers, then deciding to scatter some of their seeds in the wet earth brought me back to the physical experience of being in a body, an active participant in the life of this planet. The pointed tips of the seeds at first stuck in my fingertips, but I finally let them go to the wind, and it was like slowly releasing my need to do and accomplish more.

When our bodies and souls most ache for it, rest can feel like a kind of death, so much that we avoid the practices and tools that help us through it. I can remember coming home from a day of teaching, having commuted over an hour each way, my heart still racing, feeling rattled. But I could hardly force myself to sit down for even five minutes. When we've been going at such unnatural and unmanageable speeds, the idea of stillness feels overwhelming and even panic-inducing. Yet relief and renewal can happen in tiny doses—a short walk, a few minutes spent sitting far away from all devices, a few hours in nature or at a museum. I am always surprised, though I shouldn't be by now, how much creativity can emerge out of those spaces of radical self-care, when I offer myself the solitude that feeds me. We all desperately want to be carried home to ourselves again. So, we must listen to the necessary message of burnout when it comes for us. Our bodies will tell us what we need, and we will become like fierce warriors for our own well-being, pushing through resistance and shame to embrace the rest we crave.

INVITATION FOR WRITING & REFLECTION

Write about a time when you felt burned out and decided to make a change. What led to this feeling of burnout, and how did you embrace a new way of being in the face of stress and anxiety?

One Word I Don't Need

I am banishing the word busy
from my mind, like picking
stones from the lentils I have
just washed in the colander.
Is there an uglier word than
busy, with its two hurried
syllables and hard consonants
rushing out of the mouth?
Used mostly as an excuse
not to be where I am right now,
which is leaning over the sink
and letting lentils slide through
my fingers, feeling their smoothness
as I soften into the minutes,
no longer seeing this as a task
but simply imagining what
it will be like later to savor
the lentils after they've simmered
for hours with roasted tomatoes,
cumin, and coconut milk, when we
ladle them into waiting bowls
and silence our phones, laying them
both face down on the table.

We can grow so accustomed to busyness in our lives that, as mindfulness pioneer Jon Kabat-Zinn has pointed out, we become more like "human doings" than human beings, valuing ourselves only for what we produce, accomplish, or cross off our to-do lists.

We must often make a conscious effort to halt the momentum of doing and tend to the deeper "being" part of our human selves, which delights in small things, even rinsing a colander-full of red lentils and picking out each of the tiny stones. Or sitting down to a home-cooked meal with our family and friends. We tend to our souls most by slowing down, and doing our best to find those gaps in the day when we can be wholly present to what we are already doing. We long to feel useful and a part of something that is larger than ourselves, yet the danger lies in using busyness as an excuse not to be here, telling ourselves we are too busy for the joy and play that refresh our spirits.

I lived like this for several years, until I heard the poet Naomi Shihab Nye say that she had stopped using the word "busy," banishing it from her vocabulary. She realized that it had become a barrier to saying "yes" to life, and often led to a sense of scarcity, feeling that there simply wasn't enough time in the day. I do my best to live without using the word "busy," yet I honor how challenging it can be, especially for people who care for children or loved ones. The hours of every day can feel so crowded, it seems there's no room to stop and savor a task so much that it becomes more of a blessing. When I'm caught in busyness, I try to check in with my body and see where I might be clenched or tight. Often, I am holding in my stomach, or my heart is thumping wildly, sure signs that I'm rushing through life just to get to the next thing that must be done. I relax those tense muscles when I can, take a deep breath, and remind myself that I'm not just doing, I am also being. Somehow, it helps to know that I can call on this deeper part of myself, whether I'm rinsing lentils, opening a can of coconut milk, or checking my work email one more time before dinner. Then I can place the phone face down on the table and settle my attention on the bowl in front of me, on my husband across the table, on the world I want to live in.

INVITATION FOR WRITING & REFLECTION

Is there some task or chore that you secretly love doing and that brings you into a more settled and centered space? Describe it in every delicious detail, relishing all of the sensory images.

From Doing to Being

I stopped making coffee, put down the grinder
and turned to the kitchen window
to watch bats in the backyard swooping
through dawn-blue air in some looping
formation known only to them.

I had to stand still for several minutes
before I saw the gnats they feed on
rising like dust motes from their beds
between blades of unmown grass
into the hour of their deaths.

It was a kind of dying for me too
as I moved from doing to being, human
to animal simply there and breathing,
watching the bats, loop by loop,
unstitching darkness from the dawn sky.

It happened in the way of most mindful moments on an otherwise ordinary day.

I had woken up early to make coffee when out of the corner of my eye, I noticed dark blurs circling back and forth in the yard just beyond our kitchen window. I had no choice but to stop what I was doing—not wanting to make any extra noise—and watch those beings as they fed on insects I could not see, rising up from the grass at that early hour. I say it was a kind of dying because the voices in my head, the task list I was already going over for the day—all of it just faded away, and I was reborn into a few awestruck moments of fuller presence. I had seen the occasional bat in our backyard before, but never so many, and never flying in a looping formation like that, so coordinated and intentional it seemed they were fulfilling their own morning ritual. Though it can take something we've never seen or noticed to draw us out of the stream of our constant thinking, we have the choice to stop what we're doing at any time and look more closely at the people and the world around us. We move into presence simply by being there and breathing, feeling ourselves a part of the natural order of things again.

INVITATION FOR WRITING & REFLECTION

Can you think back to a moment when you gave yourself permission to stop what you were doing and enter the space of non-doing? What did you notice when you stopped? Describe what you saw and felt in that moment of being, when the typical concerns and stories of the mind fell away.

Self-Compassion

My friend and I snickered the first time
we heard the meditation teacher, a grown man,
call himself *honey*, with a hand placed
over his heart to illustrate how we too
might become more gentle with ourselves
and our runaway minds. It's been years
since we sat with legs twisted on cushions,
holding back our laughter, but today
I found myself crouched on the floor again,
not meditating exactly, just agreeing
to be still, saying *honey* to myself each time
I thought about my husband splayed
on the couch with aching joints and fever
from a tick bite—what if he never gets better?—
or considered the threat of more wildfires,
the possible collapse of the Gulf Stream,
then remembered that in a few more minutes,
I'd have to climb down to the cellar and empty
the bucket I placed beneath a leaky pipe
that can't be fixed until next week. How long
do any of us really have before the body
begins to break down and empty its mysteries
into the air? *Oh, honey,* I said—for once
without a trace of irony or blush of shame—
the touch of my own hand on my chest
like that of a stranger, oddly comforting
in spite of the facts.

Poet and farmer Wendell Berry once wrote: "Be joyful, though you have considered the facts."

Yet with our packed schedules, and so much negativity and injustice in the world, it can be difficult to believe we deserve any of the daily joys that actually renew us. We forget that the practice of self-compassion makes us more available to our loved ones and larger community, giving them permission to listen to their own needs as well. This dawned on me recently during a week when it seemed everything was going wrong, and so much needed doing. Brad had contracted a tick-borne illness and needed constant tending, we'd discovered water covering the floor of the cellar from a leaky pipe, and the news of damage to the natural world had become alarming, to say the least. Yet a scene came back to me from when I was first learning to meditate, when I still felt cynical and dubious about any kind of spiritual practice. My good friend and I found ourselves snickering at the meditation teacher seated on his cushion in front of the class, placing a hand on his chest and calling himself honey, as he modeled a more gentle way to approach our runaway minds and the inner critics that can keep us from doing what we love. As I worried about Brad and the state of our world, any resistance I felt toward self-compassion simply fell away. I sat still, placing a hand over my heart and letting the kicked-up dust of my own fears slowly settle inside. I now believe that if we want to see a kinder, more just world, the most reasonable place to begin is by showing kindness and sweetness to ourselves, even if it means stepping into discomfort, even if it means saying, "Oh, honey," now and then, offering ourselves the kind of warmth we often give so freely to others.

INVITATION FOR WRITING & REFLECTION

Can you remember a time when you practiced compassion and gentleness with yourself, in spite of your own discomfort and doubt? How did that outpouring of self-care affect you?

When Fear Takes Over

Never underestimate the power
of your own gentle hand
when placed over a racing heart,
that press of flesh to flesh
which says: Yes, you will make it
through this. Walk alone
in the snowy woods and listen
for the way trees speak
to each other in winter, rubbing
bare limbs together. Reach out
to a friend, let their voice
be the lullaby you never heard
as a child. Let kind words
wrap around you like a blanket
so thick it soaks up the sound
of every secret worry
spoken to the air.

Fear can cloud even the clearest of hearts, and what seems to dispel it is only softness and a gentle patience with ourselves.

When I wrote this poem, I'd been feeling fear and doubt as I entered a vulnerable new phase of my creativity, trying new things for the first time and worrying about how they might be received. It can be easy to forget how difficult it is to take a risk, creative or otherwise, and to share that work in a more public way. Though I struggled at first, I felt grateful that I had a daily writing practice and good friends who could help see me through this period. Writing this poem, first to help myself and then as an offering to others who might be going through something similar, also drove home for me the power of self-compassion, weaving such care into every corner of our own lives. We are never truly alone during these trying times, and even if someone is not physically there to comfort us, science reassures: Just our own hand placed over the heart, skin to skin, releases as much oxytocin in the body as a hug from a loved one. When faced with vulnerability and the exposure that comes of change and transition, we can retreat into old habits of coping, trying to escape the raw feelings, burying them for later. Or we can do our best to stay with them, practicing the kind of radical self-care in which we bring comfort to ourselves by any means necessary, seeking tenderness wherever we can find it, even in the touch of our own hand as we release "every secret worry" into the air around us.

INVITATION FOR WRITING & REFLECTION

What helps you loosen the grip of fear and anxiety and access your own courage again? What are some of the fears you were dealing with at the time, or that are arising right now? You might write a kind of instructional poem, directing it toward yourself, so that you can remember the most useful practices when fear takes over or you lose heart again in the future.

Losing Heart

It's not like misplacing the car keys
or forgetting your mother's address.
You know it's impossible to actually lose
the heart working so hard in the chest,
resting for only the slimmest of instants
between beats. Yet you wake some days
patting empty pockets, digging through
every drawer in the house, searching
under the bed and couch. In the space
of a night, the hope that burned bright—
flowing like a medicine in your veins—
can drain from the body, leaving you
bereft in bed and getting up only
to bathe yourself in the sickly light
of the fridge, the glow of screens.
Yet you can trust that the heart never
goes far, never abandons you for longer
than you can handle. You might be
driving to work one stormy morning,
scowling at every car that passes you
when it happens again—that sudden
leap in the chest as you see the rain-
slick blacktop shining blue in places
where it gives back the sky, and then
you're anchored again in that faithful
rhythm by which you love the world.

This poem came to me as a gift at the end of a very difficult day.

I was driving the same stale, hour-long route that morning to a job where I had never felt valued or respected by colleagues. I loved the students I was teaching, but the long commute each way in traffic, and the disconnect from co-workers sent me home each night feeling empty and dissatisfied. I was quickly losing heart and wondering if I'd ever get it back, when the smallest of miracles happened. Even though I didn't want to be where I was, driving in the aftermath of a winter storm, I noticed something. Each of the puddles held in dips in the asphalt, where potholes had been filled in, reflected back a striking blue sky that had at last overtaken the gray. I looked up and then down again at those patches of blue, feeling what I can only describe as delight—that "faithful rhythm" by which we each come to love the world. It did not fix my situation, of course, but accessing a sense of child-like wonder made life, and that day at least, much more livable. If nothing else, a mindful moment like this can remind us that the world is here, just waiting a heartbeat away for us to notice and appreciate its many small offerings—to feel the whole-body thrill of being brought back to the present and out of the trap of the thinking mind. In that more fertile and compassionate heart-space, we are able to stay open to the daily miracles that find us. By loving the world at hand, we also come to love ourselves and our own place in it.

INVITATION FOR WRITING & REFLECTION

Describe what it feels like when you "lose heart." Can you recall a specific instance when some bit of beauty or surprising sight outside of yourself brought you back to the present and inspired you, reconnecting you with your body and a sense of greater compassion for yourself and the world?

Beech Trees in Spring

I want to be like the maples,
letting go so easily of their leaves
in the slightest autumn breeze,
surrendering every piece of themselves
they no longer need, and embracing bareness
like a new suit they can simply step into.
But I'm more like the beech trees,
which cling to the husks of their leaves
long into spring, refusing to give up
even a scrap of who they once were
until the last possible minute.
Perhaps they need the reassurance,
or maybe they're here to lend music
to the silence of winter, leaves
beaten thin as tissue paper rustling
a lonely chorus in the snow-covered woods—
until buds push up to the surface,
and with no other choice, they say yes
to the final scatter and release,
learning again, as if for the first time,
how loss leaves room for something new.

The truth is, very few of us can be like the maples, letting go as easily as autumn leaves.

We cling to what's familiar and predictable, believing this will help us guide and control our lives. Yet there can be so much wisdom, and even joy, in "embracing bareness," accepting the inevitable losses and transitions that come our way so that we may process them. I wrote this poem after taking a long, late winter walk through the woods, noticing the way all the beech trees still clung to their leaves, even in mid-April. Those leaves, shriveled and "beaten thin as tissue paper," still held a quiet, transcendent beauty. For a while, they appear gold at the tips of the branches, lending a little brightness to the otherwise drab and colorless winter landscape. They also offer a "lonely chorus" to anyone who's listening, their rustling often the only sound that accompanies me as I pass through the bare trees, not even a squirrel stirring in the snow. The morning after my walk, the image of those pale leaves, still attached to branches in spite of strong winds, ice storms, and the battering of sleet, came back to me over and over. I knew they must be trying to teach me something important.

I've often chided myself for staying in certain relationships or jobs for longer than I needed to, sensing the time to move on had come, but not yet wanting to upend my life and navigate the uncertain terrain that comes with change. Now, I wonder: What if the way forward in our lives seems clear only in retrospect, when we've already taken the right action, and we feel the thrill of finally growing toward a new path? What if we need to cling to certain people and things to learn our lessons most fully, to be ready for the next inevitable transition?

We know the wisdom of letting go, releasing past selves that no longer serve us. We often hold up such non-attachment as the enlightened ideal. But those beech trees seemed to preach the wisdom of holding on for as long as we need to, not trying to force our growth, or rush off in some new direction too soon. We don't often make essential changes in our lives until the last possible minute, when there's no longer any other choice. Such is the power of predictability and comfort. Yet none of us should feel the pressure to let go of anything or forgive anyone before we are absolutely ready. I've heard from friends deep in grief about the cruelty of others who believe they should have moved on from sorrow by now, who think less of them for staying in the tangle of emotions and welcoming each one. As author and rest coach Octavia Raheem has written: "Joy is an act of rebellion. And so is allowing ourselves to feel our grief." We can forgive ourselves for the human need to hold on for however long we need to, no matter how many seasons it takes for us to let go and move on.

INVITATION FOR WRITING & REFLECTION

Describe a time in your life when in retrospect you can see that you held onto something or someone longer than it seemed you needed to. Do you find some teacher in the natural world for embracing what arises and letting go when the time is right?

Consider the Lilies

This is the unbreaking news:
today on my walk I saw
hundreds of trout lilies
breaking through leaf litter,
their spotted green leaves—
nearly translucent in the sun—
pointed upward like spears,
already turning the leftovers
of this last difficult year
into fertilizer, into food.
Consider these lilies, how
they'd never call themselves
broken simply because they
had to live in darkness
and cold for months, how
they don't have to be told
to reach for the dappled light
they know they need to bloom.

When we're feeling the pull of too many obligations
or the despair of having absorbed too much
disturbing news on a given day, it can be useful
to step out of our usual routines and into
whatever nature is available.

On the morning I describe here, I had decided to go for a walk in a
local nature preserve I don't often frequent, and much to my delight,
in spite of the chilly and gray day, I noticed hundreds of wildflowers
known as trout lilies sprouting up between tree trunks in the leaf
litter everywhere I stepped. Somehow, the persistence of these small
beings, returning yet again after a long winter and pushing their way
up toward the light, gave me a profound sense of release, as I struggled to push through my own depression and anxiety. I don't claim
that a dose of nature can "cure" us of any difficulties, yet as someone
who's suffered with anxiety his whole life, I can say from years of
experience that when I am able to give my attention to something or
someone else outside of myself for a sustained period, I simply feel
better. I notice, too, that my self-talk starts to change. For instance,
though I had been feeling broken that winter by a difficult year of
caregiving several loved ones, somehow the trout lilies gave me hard
evidence, as nature often does, that just because we might have
to live in darkness and cold for months doesn't mean that we are
broken. Just because we're depressed doesn't mean we won't reach
for the light we need when the time is right for us to emerge again.

INVITATION FOR WRITING & REFLECTION

Take a walk or hike or make a circuit around the yard, bringing a notebook with you. Pause and see what living thing calls to your attention, listening deeply for any words or lines that come to you. What evidence of gentle persistence can you find in the natural world?

Self-Love

Treat yourself as an honored guest
in your own home. Sweep the floors,
whisking loose hairs and crumbs
into the dustpan, clearing cobwebs
as if you are about to arrive here
for the first time. Stoke the fire
in the wood stove, stacking logs
of maple and birch, whose bark
curls into flames that will warm
the whole house as you step inside
your body, learning to love its shape
like never before. Offer yourself
the wedge of brie you've been keeping
in the back of the fridge, pop open
whatever bottle you've been saving
for the moment you finally become
your own dream date, your own
special occasion. Now sit at the table
set for one, and feast on a simple
meal of bread and cheese, relishing
each taste of this new life, which has
always been waiting inside you.

The late Vietnamese Buddhist monk Thich Nhat Hanh once wrote: "To revere each other is to treat each other at all times as an honored guest."

This is the path toward greater tenderness and connection; but how can we treat others as honored guests, if we can't first do the same for ourselves? I began this poem with the images of carefully cleaning and preparing the house as I often do when someone is about to arrive and stay over. Yet one day, as I swept, dusted, and vacuumed, it occurred to me: Why don't I clean and tidy for myself, too? I take such pleasure in an orderly house, everything in its place, and feel that my own thoughts become more ordered as well. Yet I don't usually offer this kindness to myself, as if I were my own honored guest. As the poem went on, and as I allowed the images to unfold on their own, it dawned on me how much I hold back, how I believe that certain "treats" are only appropriate for special occasions and not for everyday use. How many of us do the same, saving the good stuff for others, our partner, or family members—when we could just as easily become our own dream date, our own special occasion, indulging in what we sincerely love? We are sometimes afraid of appearing too selfish, though we could let that word take on a more positive meaning. What if we encouraged each other to be more selfish, in the sense of nourishing our self with the joy we so often think must be reserved for others? What if we indulged in the things that called to us, letting our child-selves guide us now and then toward small delights we might have forgotten, believing they are no longer appropriate for us as adults.

Self-love is a reflection of the honor and reverence we choose to pay to ourselves. Yet we don't achieve true self-love overnight, especially if we lead hectic lives and take care of others—partners, children, ailing parents—day in and day out. We have to start with the smallest and most tender of ways we might show ourselves the love we give freely to others, the love that we may not have felt growing up. I learned at an early age, for instance, to turn off my desires, to tell myself "no" before even asking, because we often didn't have the money for extras in my family. No to the packet of chocolate doughnuts at the checkout; no to the piano and French lessons I deeply wanted; no to school trips and playing in band because you had to buy or rent the instruments. It has been a healing process for me to take a step back from that way of being in the world and begin to say "yes" to what calls to me again. This has been especially true in my own writing practice, to which I have said "yes" every day that I can over the years, even when others might have given up. I trust that, even if I don't "produce" something every time I sit down at my desk, I am still taking care of myself in ways that others could not. It's never too late to start saying yes to self-love, when we can see it as something more essential to our well-being, revealing the truer life that's always been waiting inside us.

INVITATION FOR WRITING & REFLECTION

How might you treat yourself as an honored guest in your own home? How might you express self-love in more nourishing and indulgent ways? You may want to write a set of instructions to yourself that you can return to later at those times when self-love feels inaccessible.

Unlocking the Heart

Try to love what holds you back,
the barred door, the padlock
firmly fastened. You may feel stuck,
but the more you love the lock
that keeps you here, the more you learn
its intricate machinery, movement
of the tumblers inside which answer
to only a certain key. Maybe a single
word could free you, maybe you have
held the key all along, stored in
the intricate machinery of your heart,
which is more than willing to open
if spoken to in just the right way.

Mark Nepo has said, "What's in the way is the way."
In other words, what blocks our path also has
to be tended before we can move forward.

We might want to go around, or turn back and find another way, but whatever blocks the heart in one place is likely to show up again in another. So much shuts us down, threatens to close us off from the world. Yet why not learn to "love the lock," and get to know what seems to keep us from the freedom we deserve? If it's true that just a few words can lock the heart, then it's also true that the smallest shift within us might be the key that opens us again to all the abundance and creativity around us. When I'm "down in my heart," feeling confused and confounded, I can convince myself there is no way out. When I feel blocked in my writing and uninspired by life, I tell myself the false story that this is how it will always be. But I have been shown countless times over the years that my own heart often holds the keys to release me from whatever prison I'm in. It's usually a matter of staying with what's in the way and waiting until a little space appears.

On the creative and spiritual path, we are going to encounter roadblocks time and again. Fear and doubt will shut us down, make us feel there is no way out. When this happens, as it does to all of us, I have found it most useful to label the fearful thoughts as they arise, naming them to myself first, and then out loud to someone I trust. Such emotions rarely survive when brought into the light of day, so that even just writing them down in a journal, and being honest about what's holding us back, has the effect of stripping fear of all its power. By labeling exactly what's going on inside us, we are able to release the emotions and free ourselves. By naming, and even welcoming, what we feel—by loving what's in the way—we find the keys that have been waiting right here inside us, ready to unlock the door.

INVITATION FOR WRITING & REFLECTION

Often, our blockages simply crave a bit of kindness and love, an acknowledgment that they are real. What's blocking you right now, keeping things from moving through? Has there been a time when you were able to unlock the heart with certain practices or rituals that you found healing?

PART THREE

Poems for Grief and Healing

On the days the pain feels everlasting,
just remember that even the most mighty storm
must eventually break to let the light through.

—Nikita Gill

Learning to Stay

I'd rather run away, but today
I give in to grief, decide to stay.
Not because I love the pain,
but because I trust what happens
when the eyes have been rinsed,
how the world begins to shimmer
like the yard after a storm:
every leaf on the maple polished,
every yellow and pink petal
brighter once the burst
of battering rain has passed.

Giving in to grief means leaving room in daily life for the inconvenience and discomfort of that universal ache.

The tears, the fear, the heat of anger—I try to let it all pass through, and often feel a little better afterward. Whatever emotion arises in us wants to be released, like rain from a storm-heavy cloud. No matter how difficult it is to yield to the pain, despite our fear that it might last forever, when we learn to stay, we are often rewarded with a glimpse of a world that shimmers with holiness. Perhaps it's because we remember again how briefly we inhabit these bodies, sharing space with each other on this planet. For a few minutes maybe, we see things with eyes rinsed clean by a sudden burst of grief. Now, as we look at the garden, the black-eyed Susans and coneflowers appear brighter, yellow and pink petals seeming to glow. Now, the leaves of each maple vibrate with the life-force we easily forget inhabits all beings.

When my mother was still alive, I once asked if she ever wept for my father, who died when they were both in their forties. "I cry a little," she said. "But I'm afraid that once I start, I won't be able to stop." I understand her fear more than ever, but she became someone who held in *all* her pain, who never gave it a chance to cycle through. On my better days, I see grief as nothing more than a necessary but passing storm. I can choose to block it, deny it, hold it in, and let it live inside the body—or I can give myself over to it completely, so that it may do its work. I can also live for that moment the tears stop flowing and the love I released seems to seep into the world all around me.

INVITATION FOR WRITING & REFLECTION

What does it feel like when you give in to your grief, staying long enough so that it may pass through? What images come to mind when you consider how the pain of loss works in us? You might begin by writing, "I give in to grief . . ." and see what arises in your heart and mind.

Tomatoes

When I bite into the bruise-
colored flesh of this heirloom tomato
known as a Cherokee Purple,
I'm transported back to the dirt road
that ran along the Meramec River
where my father pulled over
at the farm stand, then stepped out
of the truck, brushed for a moment
in gravel dust suspended in the sun.
He came back grinning, gripping
a bag of homegrown Beefsteaks so fat
they were already bursting their juices
through the brown paper, running
down his long-gone hands, which I am
reaching out to touch again before
he turns the key in the ignition,
begging him not to go, not just yet,
as I salt the next slice.

We can bring our loved ones back to life, even
if briefly, by observing small rituals like the
one I describe in this poem.

Every summer, as tomatoes ripen on their vines, I make the
time to eat one alone, salting the slices as my father once did
and remembering him back into the present moment with me.
Tomatoes were one of his favorite things in the world, and he
never passed up the chance to enjoy one. I'll never forget the day
he and I were driving back from the hospital, before the worst
of his Hepatitis C had begun to take its toll on his body. Without
warning, he pulled off on a dirt road near the Meramec River and
parked next to a farmstand I hadn't even noticed. I can still see
him stepping out into the cloud of gravel dust our truck kicked
up, then coming back a few minutes later with a bag of Beefsteak
tomatoes so juicy they were leaking through the brown paper
onto his hands. But what I recall most clearly, what returns to
me each time I bite into the first Cherokee Purple of the season,
is the innocent, childlike smile that spread across his face. He
could have shut down to life as soon as he received the difficult
diagnosis, but he kept embracing joy, even in the midst of worry,
even in the midst of extreme pain. His smile never fails to remind
me of the brevity of this one life. It reinforces the necessity of
relishing our simple joys, and of being vulnerable enough to share
such unguarded happiness with the ones we love. When we allow
ourselves to feel our joy fully, we teach others to do the same.

INVITATION FOR WRITING & REFLECTION

Describe how a lost loved one still comes back to you. Do you remember them when you eat certain foods they loved, or visit a particular place? How could you make it a regular practice to bring back someone you dearly miss, perhaps finding them in a favorite scent or in an activity they loved to do?

Telling My Father

I found him on the porch that morning,
sipping cold coffee, watching a crow
dip down from the power line into the pile
of black bags stuffed in the dumpster
where he pecked and snagged a can tab,
then carried it off, clamped in his beak
like the key to a room only he knew about.
My father turned to me then, taking in
the reek of my smoke, traces of last night's
eyeliner I decided not to wipe off this time.
Out late was all he said. And then smiled,
rubbing the small of my back through the robe
for a while, before heading inside, letting
the storm door click shut behind him.
Later, when I stepped into the kitchen,
I saw it waiting there on the table—a glass
of orange juice he had poured for me and left
sweating in a patch of sunlight so bright
I couldn't touch it at first.

Sometimes, the smallest gestures of love
become healing balms that we carry with
us for decades to come.

One of my greatest regrets is that I never came out to my father
before he passed away. I felt this ache for a long time, believing
he never truly knew me, until I realized there was actually a
moment when I'd chosen to reveal myself to him. In return, he
gave me his total acceptance and acknowledgment. This is the
scene I describe in the poem, and the process of re-creating it
allowed me to forgive myself for never actually saying the words
out loud to him, for hiding that essential part of who I am. As I
have written over and over about the last moments my father and
I shared together, I now realize he probably knew about me for a
very long time, as parents often do. Through years of grief, I also
began to see how lucky I was to experience so many moments
of exchange with this first man I loved, and how our intimacy
allowed us to communicate, without saying a thing. Most of us
have shared at least a moment or two like this with someone we
love, when we performed some silent act of service for them, or
received a sudden gift. Every relationship is complicated beyond
measure, yet there are times when we see and feel clearly enough
to know what we need to offer. There are times when we tell
someone who we are, and they embrace us, without trading even
a single word.

INVITATION FOR WRITING & REFLECTION

Have you had a moment of exchange like this, when you did something for someone else, or received their gesture of love, even if you didn't realize what was happening at the time?

Orbit

Go where it's warm
is perhaps the best advice
we can offer each other
in times of distress—
a pair of arms held out
in the hospital room,
or mugs of mint tea
taken together at the table
of mourning. You feel it
as a force field, an orbit
you slip into as soon
as you meet someone new
and sense that small,
blazing star pulsing
in their chest, drawing
you closer until you know
you'll be circling that
source of light and heat
for the rest of your life.

Times of distress, loss, or difficulty tend to lead us to those people who can offer us comfort when we need it the most.

I'd heard this advice several times—"Go where it's warm," which I took to mean: follow your instincts and move toward what brings you an undeniable sense of warmth and connection. So often, we pursue the things and people we believe we *should*, seldom stopping to ask ourselves, until perhaps grief has sapped all our patience: Do I feel warmth from this person or situation? Do I feel cared for and embraced? The body is always a reliable indicator, whether we're talking about the kind of work we want to do, the friendships we want to keep, or the partners we want to be with. Loss has a way of breaking down what felt so comfortable and true for us before, and revealing those weak places in our lives where we are missing the light we need.

Why not allow ourselves to be drawn into the orbit of people and pursuits that bring us happiness and well-being? Each of us has probably had the disconcerting experience of sensing when someone cannot show up for us, when they have no desire or ability to lift us up. They may say all the right things and put on a smile, but we come away from such interactions feeling drained or confused. The fatigue of loss offers us a way forward now, since we cannot afford to keep those relationships going anymore. We see how limited both our time and energy are, and we must decide how to spend them wisely in the years we have left. Earth circles the sun because of the life it gives, because the planet needs its light and heat to survive. The same is true of the people in our lives. A few will hopefully become suns for us, and when we feel the bloom of that warmth in our bodies, we can choose to say a resounding yes, knowing that we deserve to live in the orbit of such kindness and compassion.

INVITATION FOR WRITING & REFLECTION

Think back to a difficult time when you were drawn to someone else's warmth, when you let yourself slip into their orbit. How did this person make you feel cared for and supported? How might this help you seek out what you need right now?

Mother and Son

Though you're gone now,
my body still remembers
being held by you that evening,
wearing my blue fleece pajamas
with a white owl on the front,
and you saying, "Who, who,"
over and over, both of us laughing
as you explained that's the sound
owls make when they need
to find each other in the darkness
before sleep, a way of saying:
I can't see you, but I know
you must be there.

This poem was born after looking at an old photograph of my mother and my younger self that I keep on our refrigerator.

Suddenly, the sentence came to me in a flash: "My body still remembers being held by you." These words seemed to unlock some deeply held grief that had not yet been released, and the rest of the poem flowed from that open place in the heart as I leaned over the kitchen counter, scribbling down the lines, wiping at my eyes. The lesson of this piece, for me, is that our bodies hold onto and store all the grief, fear, and trauma we have experienced, as science has now confirmed. Yet we forget that we can also still access the past joy, light, and love of certain moments from our lives. Looking at that photo of me at two years old, wearing my blue pajamas with the owl on the front, my mother and I both laughing as she pressed me to her chest, I found that I could still recall that evening from over forty years ago. Some part of me was still laughing and smiling with innocent joy as my father snapped the photo. In spite of the pain of having lost them both, I could still feel the love of my parents encircling me, knowing they are with me even now, in the darkness of my grief, when I feel most alone.

Writing this short and simple poem about very complex feelings showed me the importance of staying true to family stories that come to define who we are and how we move through the world. When we honor past experiences, no matter how slight or simple they might seem, we stay in conversation with what Mark Nepo has called "the miracle of being." We understand that every moment of connection and love can shape us, and even re-shape us each time we bring it up from the deep well of memory. I came across the snapshot that sparked this poem while going through my mother's apartment just after she had passed. I can't explain the power that image held over me, how it called to me right away, as if I could slip right back into my two-year-old self and feel the ease of that time again. Perhaps this speaks to the power of writing, too, the necessity of following our creativity wherever it chooses to take us. I would never have guessed that I still possessed such a body-memory of being held by my mother, yet as those first words flowed through me, I knew it was absolutely true that this moment had never left me. Grief stays with us, but so does love, like two sides of the same river we are always swimming between.

INVITATION FOR WRITING & REFLECTION

Write about a time that your body still recalls, especially holding onto the love and joy you felt with a loved one who may no longer be with you. You might begin with the phrase, "My body still remembers . . ." and see what details arise for you.

Valentine

I keep thinking of the Valentine's card
my mother cut out of construction paper
and left on my bed with several chocolate
kisses taped to the back. I came home
from school that day to her sheepish face
as she told me there was something waiting
for me upstairs. *It's not much*, she said,
and in truth, I was expecting something
more dramatic than a handwritten card
with roses and hearts drawn on the front.
But I pretended to be excited, gave her
a hug, and shrugged it off when she
shook her head and said, *I feel silly now.*
A mother shouldn't do this for her son.
Her cheeks turning red as I propped
the card on my nightstand, unwrapped
the silver foil from each of the kisses,
and popped them into my mouth without
stopping to savor the sweetness
of what she had done.

A few years before she died, my mother confessed to me with a quivering voice: "I always tried to give you and your brother as much love as possible because I never had enough growing up."

When she said that, I instantly flashed back to one Valentine's Day when I came home from school with my brother, Ron, our backpacks stuffed with candy and cards from the other kids in class. My mother's bright face told of her excitement as she opened the door for us. I could tell she was hiding something. "I've got a surprise for you guys," she said, then looked away, almost sheepish. "You'll probably think I'm crazy." My brother and I bounded upstairs to our rooms and found on each of our beds a homemade Valentine's Day card from her with some chocolate Hershey kisses she must have saved for this occasion. We went back down and thanked her, gave her a peck on the cheek.

She rolled her eyes at her gesture that day, but I have never forgotten the effort she must have put into making cards with construction paper and markers because she couldn't drive down to the drug store to buy the real thing. Looking back now, of course, her cards and chocolate kisses are worth far more to me. Having heard this cherished story, my husband did something similar for me a few Valentine's Days ago when I had to work until late in the evening. I came home to find a glint in his eyes, not unlike my mother's, as he greeted me at the door and said there was a little something waiting for me upstairs. On our bed, I found ten of my favorite candy bars arranged in the shape of a giant heart with a homemade, hand-colored card resting in the middle.

These gifts remind me that showing love for one another means risking feeling silly, being judged, or being seen as sentimental. Yet isn't it always worth the risk? No matter how uncomfortable we might feel in the moment of giving—leaving a poem on the fridge for a lover, or sneaking a note into our child's lunch bag— these gestures always stay with us long after the fact.

INVITATION FOR WRITING & REFLECTION

Can you think of a time that someone surprised you with something that seemed a little sentimental, or even trivial at first, but that you ultimately never forgot? Was there a moment when you reached out to a loved one, showing your affection, and taking the risk that they might not reciprocate?

After Surgery

My mother was still getting dressed
when I stepped into the room.
She moved gingerly, wincing even
as she fumbled with the buttons
on her blouse. But her face lit up
when she saw me come to take her
home: *There's my baby*, she whispered,
then asked if I could help put on
her socks and shoes. As I knelt,
coaxing the white cotton over her
delicate ankles, a wave of grief
passed through me, for the son
I once was and never would be again.
I had to grip one of the chair legs
just to keep myself steady, and then
I did what was asked, easing her feet
into sneakers and tying the laces
in double-knots so they might never
come undone.

If we are lucky, memories of a lost loved one will soon bubble to the surface, helping to erase some of the difficult images of their final days.

It helps to embrace and explore such remembrances when they come because they create a whole picture of the loved one for us, in both heart and mind. Even if it is just a single instance, like the one I share here, you can dive deep into that scene and relish all the details of that time. This poem arrived for me years after the actual trip to the hospital that first inspired it, when my mother had the first of several hernia surgeries. I'd been worried for her, sitting for hours in the waiting room and watching her name flash on a screen that finally told me she'd been moved to Recovery. When I could finally see her, she greeted me with words that nearly broke my heart open: "There's my baby." She never stopped calling me that either, no matter how old I was. She never stopped feeling that I was her child, even as she became the one who needed the most attention and care.

What broke me open the most was when my mother asked me to put on her socks and lace up her sneakers. As soon as I heard her raspy, child-like voice, the knowledge flashed through me that, from now on, I would be more like a parent in our rela-tionship. I did my best to hold it together as I knelt there on the floor, pulling the cotton socks onto her feet, then sliding them into her shoes. It still seems a miracle to me now, reading these words again, that I can access what I felt in the moment. Though it happened several years ago, I could step into that sunlit room again, breathe in the scents of disinfectant, feel the fraying laces of her shoes in my fingers as I tied them in double-knots so they would not come undone.

As Native American author Robin Wall Kimmerer has written, "Maybe there is no such thing as time, only moments each with their own story." Don't we hold onto the stories of our own vivid moments more than anything else, with their seeds of meaning, and all the riches they contain? In a way, I think of this poem as a blessing, both for my mother and myself, and for every child who's ever had to look after a parent or guardian. The closeness of our whole relationship is held inside the single, loving gesture of a son helping his mother get dressed again after surgery. And because I chose to preserve the story of this moment, now that my mother is gone, I can relive it as often as I wish, kneeling before her again, feeling the sweetness of her gratitude, knowing I did all I could to care for her while she was here.

INVITATION FOR WRITING & REFLECTION

Time-travel back to a moment that you want to preserve, perhaps when you were taking care of a loved one, and sensed that you would want to return to this scene later. Write down all the things you still recall about the memory, every gesture, every sensory detail that now feels sacred to you.

Little Altars Everywhere

There are little altars everywhere
in the world, places where you can
lay down your suffering for a while.
Hollowed-out oak trunk by the forest trail
where you leave acorns and pine cones
and worries you've gathered on a cushion
of moss, whose patience softens everything.
Or the bench at the busy intersection
where streams of people crossing the street
parted around you, and you fell in love
with each of them—the men in suits, babies
strapped in strollers—and left your fear
crumpled there like a useless receipt.
Or the shelf where you keep the box
of your mother's ashes next to an electric
candle that flickers day and night, how you
give your grief to the yellow glow of that
false flame over and over, knowing
that even the plainest of light can be
enough sometimes to hold your pain.

We can always find places to lay down our pain and suffering for a while, no matter how heavy or impossible it might feel.

I wrote this poem one rainy day while walking to the mailbox at the end of our dirt road, realizing that with each step, each tree I passed, I was shedding bits of grief over the loss of my mother. I tend not to work from ideas, but instead wait for the call of language, a string of words to capture my attention and feed the spark of inspiration. But there was something about the notion of "little altars everywhere," which enticed me as the phrase swept into my mind. It occurred to me that this is what we do while writing: We take some plain and seemingly ordinary scene or image from our everyday lives, and we lay it on the altar of our close attention, not so much to worship, but to welcome what insights it brings. Whether on the page or out in the world, there are makeshift altars where we can abandon our fears and worries for a while, handing them over to some larger force that we don't need to name or understand to trust that it is there. My poetry professor in college, David Clewell, always said to us: "Poetry is much bigger than the poet." Creativity is a much more powerful force than that of the individual creator, and I love the idea that when we sit down to write something, when we paint or sculpt or cook or follow our creative spirit in any number of ways, we enter a sacred space. In fact, each thing we make that did not exist before becomes a kind of altar that is now accessible and useful to others.

We are not searching for the kind of ornate, opulent altars we might in churches and cathedrals, though those are beautiful, too. Instead, let's seek out everyday altars—tree trunks, benches, and shelves in our homes where we come to worship in our own personal ways. If we approach our creative and spiritual lives with reverence, then nothing is separate, nothing is ordinary. Every moment turns into a church we step into when we decide to release our suffering, even for a few seconds, and pay attention to what calls to us, what brings us joy and relief, or allows us to feel a greater sense of connection with the world around us. As Naomi Shihab Nye has said: "Your life is the poem." We are always living into our creations and letting them guide us toward the most honest and wholehearted versions of ourselves. Our life becomes what we create, and we are healed each time we find signs of the sacred in our everyday lives.

INVITATION FOR WRITING & REFLECTION

Where have you found some of your own little altars in the world, holy places where you return to lay down your pain for a while? Can you describe a few moments when you were able to release your pain and give it over to some force larger than you? You might begin with the phrase, "I give my grief to . . ." and repeat it as many times as necessary.

Light and Dark

Half-awake, I lose myself in a pool
of late morning sun and leaf shadows
flashing on the floor outside my bedroom,
what the Japanese call *komorebi*—light
and dark held in the same container
of a single moment, as we hold them in us,
learning to love equally a burst of joy
welling up like wind in the crowns of trees
and a sorrow that still weighs us down
like stones in the shoes, like swallowed clay.
Today, I stand here at the edge of both,
knowing that if I want to walk in the light
I'll have to dance with the shadows too.

It can feel as if we carry two heartbeats within us—
sorrow and joy, grace and grief always intertwining,
falling into a common music we each must live by.

I still recall the day that led to this poem, when I woke feeling
exhausted with a pressing sense of overwhelm. I had taken on too
much work and was also trying to look after my mother from a
distance, being sure she was taking her medication and receiving
the care she needed each day. Her several illnesses kept growing
worse, and now she was also grieving the loss of her own mother,
who had died a month before. Every day during this difficult
period become a dance between taking care of myself and tending others, trying to embrace my own joy, while also looking after
the pain and needs of my loved ones and co-workers. One morning, having just stumbled from bed, I was stopped by a perfect
square of light on the floor, the play of leaf-shadows against a
backdrop of full sunshine. I had learned years before that the
Japanese had a word for this phenomenon—*komorebi*—but had
never witnessed such a striking example, and had certainly never
given myself permission to feel the healing effects of just standing there in the warmth and flashing light.

I'd been lost in my worries about my mother, replaying hard
conversations we'd had about her moving out of her small apartment, where she lived alone, and into a care home. I still hear
her sobs on the other end of the phone when I asked her to
consider this, and the words she kept repeating: "I can't believe

this is happening to me." Now that my mother is gone, I still feel the edginess and heartbreak of those days, of having to become the parent for her at an already crowded time in my life. Yet I can also still tap into the sensation of relief that came as I stepped into that pool of light and darkness both, the sun-warmed floor beneath my bare feet, the shadows playing across my body.

We all want to walk in the light, staying positive and loving, but our hearts by nature are containers for everything that arises in us. It took a quiet moment of *komorebi* for me to see the truth of this. If we can let ourselves welcome it all, following our joys, both large and small, and our sorrows, too, then we slip into what Trappist monk and author Thomas Merton once called the "hidden wholeness" at the center of our lives. We may not want to dance with the shadows that chase us, but refusing to do so now only ensures that they will burst to the surface later on. Perhaps the regular practice of pausing, as I did on that difficult day, can show us the authentic power of holding everything we feel at once, no matter how contradictory it might seem.

INVITATION FOR WRITING & REFLECTION

Think back to a time when you felt a burst of joy and sorrow in the same moment. How did the two seemingly opposing emotions coexist in you?

Winter Walk

Our two shadows move in tandem
on the snowy gravel road,
ice crystals forming in our beards
almost indistinguishable
from the silver beginning to show there.

Ten or even twenty years ago,
I never would have imagined
a life as intertwined as this—
words shared back and forth,
one shadow holding the other up

as clumps of snow sift down
from pines, and we stop
for the streak of a red fox
crossing the road up ahead
like a shot arrow, here then

gone in a flash. I remember
what your grandmother said
just after her husband had passed:
Relish every moment, honey.
The years go by so fast.

During a long winter walk one morning with Brad, considering our own mortality, I fell into a moment of presence that made me so grateful for my life, in spite of all the grief.

I happened to be watching the way he moved his arms and legs, the interplay of our shadows on the freshly plowed gravel roads. In the years we've been together, we've noticed the gray beginning to slip into our hair and beards, our age starting to show in the many subtle ways of the body that is always changing as time goes on. I love those times when I drop into the moment, and thoughts sift away like melting snow on the pine. Or when all the stories I tell myself dissolve entirely, as when we stopped for the rare sighting of a fox crossing the road in front of us. The red streak disappeared over the hill before my mind even registered what it was. As I considered the speed and arrow-like trajectory of the fox, as I noticed ice forming in Brad's beard, and felt the crystals in my own stubble well, I remembered what Brad's grandmother had said to us just after the passing of her beloved husband. Devastated by the loss, she gripped Brad's hand, while dabbing at her eyes, and urged him to savor every moment. Her words stay with me now that she's gone, too, and return with each fresh loss. Whether on a walk in nature or out in the world, I am learning to welcome exchanges like this, which remind me the essential skill of cultivating presence and appreciation for life in the short time that we are here.

INVITATION FOR WRITING & REFLECTION

Write about a time when you felt the full reality of time's passage, and allowed the realization of impermanence to draw you more deeply into a moment of mindfulness. Try to re-create all the sensory details that came alive for you in that instance.

PART FOUR

Poems for Mindfulness and Presence

A miracle happened:
another day of life.

—Paulo Coelho

The Present

The gift doesn't always arrive
tied with ribbon,
wrapped in tissue paper.

It can be as plain
as the glass of orange juice
your father poured for you
just before he died
and left on the kitchen table—
how you drank from it for years.

Or the rustling of cattails
in the marsh beside the road
as a muskrat slips through
that clear water
and drops you like an anchor
into the center of yourself.

It is the wool blanket
draped across your lap—
every pill of white fuzz
you pick from it when worried—
and the urge to reach out
and rub the arm of a friend
about to start radiation again.

It is the present
of enough time and space
to look into her tired face
and see the eyes of a child
staring back at you
through the fear.

Because so much of my spiritual practice revolves around doing my best to stay present, I find myself keeping an inventory of those moments when the world felt dazzlingly alive to me, when I was fully in my body and experiencing every sensation as it passed through.

In fact, you could say that is the reason I write poetry in the first place, each poem being a moment that exists outside of clock-time, condensed into a form that allows me to access it again and again when I need to remember the truth of life's brevity.

We call each moment before it passes, "the present," and it can be a gift, but only if we are there to experience it, only if we give ourselves over to it completely. Each of the images in this poem has the power to unlock the past for me, until I'm instantly transported back to that glass of orange juice my father left for me, or the muskrat sliding through the water of the pond by the side of the road where my husband and I walk in the evening. I especially remember sitting on the couch with a friend as she described the radiation she was about to begin for her cancer. She seemed detached from what was happening—a natural response—and seemed to be putting on a brave face for the world, even her close friends, instead of admitting her own vulnerabilities. That night, however, I saw through the mask she often wore to the frightened girl hidden inside. I only saw this because I was present enough, the gravity of the situation having dropped that anchor inside me until I was rooted to the space we were sharing together. I looked deeply in her eyes and knew then just how afraid she was. Not needing to say a word about what I'd seen, not needing to acknowledge her fear—and knowing that would just shut her down even more—I gave her a long hug and trusted that was enough.

INVITATION FOR WRITING & REFLECTION

Make a "presence list" of those times in your life when you felt you were wholly there, undistracted and in the moment. What images or sensations stay with you?

Night Dweller

Fear tries to keep you small,
presses you under its wide thumb

so you never want to leave the house,
make the phone call, ask for help.

But sometimes you pry yourself loose,
slip out into the winter night

and pass through a shimmering black tunnel—
no moon, no stars, no flashlight—

where anything might happen, and does;
where your body might fail you, and does.

You fall to your knees and listen
to the scuffing noise of leftover leaves

on the beech trees, calling with each rustle:
Be more like us. Dwell naked

in the night without running away.
Hear what secret languages you learn

by staying. See what sweeping thoughts
perch in each of your open branches.

Few of us speak the truth of fear, which is that it's often more comfortable to rest under its wide thumb— to stay hidden—than to step out into the open.

At certain times, we'd rather languish under the covers and suffer than ask another for help, honestly revealing the fact that we can no longer go it alone. Fear thrives on this brand of shame and tells us that if we approach those people in our lives that we look up to the most with some problem we cannot enter on our own, they will surely see us as weak, and reject us. But staying with the discomfort and anxiety, then pushing through to the other side of exposure, helps us to name fear and rob it of most of its power. As Mark Nepo has written: "The longer we resist the temptation of fear, in order to discern what is truly threatening from what is stressful or uncomfortable, the less violent our reactions are." Accepting and staying with the sticky energy of fear means we are much less likely to harm ourselves or others in a failed attempt to rid ourselves of the overwhelming feelings.

But how do we dwell naked in the night of whatever darkness might descend? How do we trust that exposing ourselves like winter trees is the right choice, when we feel so raw and vulnerable? Like anything, making peace with fear is a muscle we must strengthen and tone over time. Once we realize that we will never rid ourselves of fear altogether, but can right-size it by revealing it to ourselves and others, the process becomes easier. Then we see that fear and worry can be merely passengers who have no say in what we do or where we go next. We can pry ourselves loose from their grip and pass through that shimmering black tunnel to the other side. With fear as our silent companion, we can enter more fully the life we were meant to live.

INVITATION FOR WRITING & REFLECTION

What does fear feel like when you experience it? And what happens when it finally lifts, when you are finally able to work yourself free from its grips? You might start with the phrase "Fear tries to . . ." and allow your imagination to range free.

Selah

After black clouds swirled in the sky,
and rain made a lake of the driveway,
the early evening turned so quiet
I could hear suds dissolving in the sink
from the sponge I'd just squeezed out,
bubbles popping, draining away.
And I dropped so easily into myself
like a rock sinking through clear water,
the scribe writing the story of my life
must have decided to insert the word
selah, that appears over and over
in the Psalms, and which we can only
guess is an invitation to the reader
to pause here in the text. Leave room
between this breath and the next
for the sound of that still, small voice
rising up in you.

Each pause we take on our own behalf, especially when exhausted and in need of refueling, becomes nothing less than sacred, a deeper way of listening to ourselves.

Sometimes, even without effort, such moments will find us, like sudden gaps opening up in what had been a busy and overcrowded day. When we say "yes" to them, fully embracing the pauses, we agree to healing ourselves, little by little, from the harmful over-whelm our culture often imposes on us. The evening I capture in this poem was a plain one—just finishing up the dishes, then wash-ing lettuce and chopping carrots for a salad. But then time seemed to stretch out as I noticed the silence of the house for the first time, so quiet I could hear the bubbles from my dishwater dissolving in the sink. I felt a tiny pull of awe for that sound I had never stopped long enough to hear before, and for the clarity that came along with it. I thought of the word *selah*, which I had just encountered, and which appears at the end of several Psalms in the Bible. Though its exact origin and meaning remain a mystery, we can guess that it's a note to "stop and listen."

We absorb so much as we move through our lives, like sponges that can hold no more. And if we don't take the time to release and reflect on all that we've brought into ourselves, we end up feeling squeezed for space, out of touch with our true self. Any kind of pause or break in the day can feel holy because it allows us to see the shimmering, tangible quality of the actual, physical world again. Even an act as simple as wiping down the counters, or washing soil from the seams of a head of buttercrunch lettuce, can become a kind of ritual, if we allow a touch of mindfulness to infuse what we do. Occasionally, giving ourselves these smaller pauses—for rest, meditation, or creativity—can show us that we need a larger *selah* in our lives, perhaps a more extended period of retreat in which to listen more deeply to the inner voice we have ignored for too long. Even saying the word, *selah*, one feels the sense of an inhale and long exhale, a single full breath that, if taken consciously, allows us just a little more space in the heart and mind.

INVITATION FOR WRITING & REFLECTION

Write about your own *selah*, a time when you were able to pause deeply, and the ordinary world took on a magical, almost miraculous quality as a result. What did you notice around you, and in your own body, as you dropped into yourself?

Natural Silence

It's not easy to find the silence
behind traffic noise and the rush of a jet
dragging its contrails through the sky.
But here it is again in the in-between,
when I learn to listen long enough
to the call-and-response of birdsong,
to wind pulsing in the canopies of trees,
and every wing-flutter of the phoebe
who's built her cup of a nest out of moss
and mud beneath the eaves of our house.
I know the stillness will last for just
a few beats before the roar of a Harley
takes over, and a tractor rumbles through
the rocky field outside my window.
So I sink into it while I can, as I do into water
so clean and clear, for a moment at least
I swear I can see to the bottom of everything.

I recently returned from a long trip to Quebec City, having spent a week in that place of traffic noise, sirens, and crowds of people.

Back home, as I stepped out of my car, the sound of newly leafed-out trees greeted me, each one seeming to whisper "hello." The world itself is seldom silent or calm, yet there are these natural sounds that can bring about an inner stillness for us. When I heard the maples whispering in the wind, I felt something inside myself release, and I let out a long sigh. I am blessed to live in the woods, in a house so surrounded by trees, it sometimes feels as if we're living up in the branches themselves. Yet even I can forget the healing power of nature, the compassionate way the natural world will hold our pain with us. "Forest bathing" has now become a popular practice, and while's there's no doubt about the relief we feel while walking in the woods, we don't have to find a forest to access the natural silence I speak about in this poem. Just stepping outside in the grass or strolling in a park alone can bring us a sense of well-being, as long as we allow ourselves to receive it, as long as we are willing to listen without our usual distractions. We know "the stillness will last for just a few beats," and, so, we train ourselves to sink into such moments of silence as we would slip into a lake or river.

Placing ourselves in the arms of nature can bring us greater clarity, too, once we move beyond the sounds of our world, at last hearing past the roar of jets, motorcycles, and sirens, to a deeper place inside ourselves. Such listening is not always easy to practice. It might seem pointless at first, and we may find ourselves resisting the fuller presence because of outer and inner noise alike. But the longer we stay with the intention to tap into this compassionate natural silence, the more we receive the rewards of dropping down into the center of ourselves. We can access nature and stillness no matter where we are, and instead of treating the forest or farm fields as a museum of things we regard from afar, we might learn to immerse ourselves, throwing wide open the doors of our senses, and letting it all in—birdcall, traffic noise, and wind pulsing in the trees that seem to welcome us.

INVITATION FOR WRITING & REFLECTION

Write about your own "clean and clear" moment of natural silence, when you were able to hear past other human-made noises and sink into a place of deeper presence in nature. What gifts do your senses bring when you choose to pause and let in the world?

Message

I wanted to capture that quiet moment
after the heron splashed up from the pond,
when a pair of wings opened wide in me
and white space erased every thought I had.
I could hear bullfrogs beginning to thrum
their mud-songs, could feel the blue blades
of fescue laid down for the coming storm,
but the chirping of the phone in my pocket
broke the calm, and before the heron could
turn to a gray speck among stacked clouds,
I was thinking again, wondering who it was,
then taking out the phone, tapping its screen
aglow with the image of a yellow envelope
waiting to be opened, my moment of stillness
floating off with tufts of thistledown caught
on the wind of the world's wild mind.

We might fight to hold onto moments of calm,
when the mind has quieted enough for us to notice
the natural world and feel a real part of it again.

Yet we must accept that mindfulness—that mind-body fullness
that lets us know we're right here—can last for only so long, before
the rest of the world presses in again. I wrote this poem while
staying at a friend's farmstead in Nebraska for the summer. I didn't
often get a phone signal there, so I usually just carried my phone
around on long walks to keep track of the time. I visited a nearby
pond almost every day, but on this morning, I came upon a great
blue heron hunting in the early fog that rose up from the water. By
the time I had named that majestic bird, however, the heron had
already lifted off with a splash from the pond, shedding water from
its wide wings. This was the first time I'd ever come so close to one
of these creatures, and the motion of its upward flight made me
gasp out loud and grab my chest as we do when lifted up ourselves
and dropped back into a moment of sudden awe.

When it happened, all my thoughts stopped. I did not even have
the desire or inclination to snap a picture. But I did want to stay in the
quality of that deeper presence both in my body and in the reeds by
the pond. I now felt an instant kinship with the heron, as if once again
aware of the thinnest threads always connecting us, one to the other.
Just then, my phone must have picked up a stronger signal. It began
to buzz in my pocket and, out of habit, I took it out, looking at the lit
face even as I resented the abrupt intrusion of the message alert.

This is the truth we now live with: Most of us carry machines of distraction with us everywhere we go. Yet only we decide how much we will let them control us and the movements of our minds. I try not to carry my phone with me, especially if I'm walking in nature, but the pull remains hard to resist. I know how prone I am to distraction, and I'd rather not give my mind the chance to latch onto anything that might carry me away from what's right here. Whether it's a blue heron, a few tiger lilies blooming in the side yard, or the oil stain on the pavement at a gas station—rainbowed ripples catching the evening sun as it sets. I want to stay with what calls to me.

INVITATION FOR WRITING & REFLECTION

Describe a time when you felt dropped back into the present by some outer event or scene. How did it feel to be right there with what was happening? How long did the moment of stillness last for you?

This Now

This moment was shaped for you
like a pair of handmade shoes
that conform exactly to the curve
and arch of each tender foot.
This is the moment you move in
no matter where you go, or what
you walk across—cobblestones,
concrete, the fresh layer of snow
that snaps like bubble wrap
as you step into a warm house.
This is now the ground you were
always meant to meet, letting
your feet press against the earth
like ink-stamps leaving their mark
wherever you choose to step.

Each moment was shaped for us to feel and experience fully. Yet we often forget as we get caught up in the day's triumphs, struggles, and endless demands.

I believe that each moment we inhabit completely can stay with us for years to come, both through our memory and the strengthened habit of moving through the world with more presence and awareness.

When I was first introduced to walking meditation while on a retreat, I found the slow, mindful movements almost excruciating. I was embarrassed at the way the other attendees and I were instructed to inch forward in a circle around the grounds of the meditation center. Walking meditation is simply the act of paying deep attention to every step you take, right down to the moment your foot meets the earth. The slower the better, and it's easiest to find a patch of ground where you can walk about ten feet, then turn around, focusing your mind only on the act of walking as you might focus on the act of breathing during regular meditation.

After trying it a few more times on my own, I came to value the calming and centering effect it had on my whole being. I saw I could also carry that centeredness with me into everyday life, while climbing the stairs on a busy day at work, for instance, or while rushing out to get coffee. I would remind myself to be there for the sensation of each step. Being present to all the intricate and minute movements of my feet also became a metaphor for how I want to meet each moment, no matter where I am or what I happen to be walking on.

My affection for mindful walking only deepened when I read Buddhist monk and peace activist Thich Nhat Hanh's description in his book *The Path of Emancipation*: "When you stamp a seal onto a piece of paper," he wrote, "you make sure that the whole seal prints on the paper, so that when you remove the seal, the image is perfect. When we practice walking, we do the same thing. Every step we take is like placing a seal on the ground. Mindfulness is the ink." I still love kicking off my sandals and walking barefoot on a patch of grass still damp with dew. I love hearing the snow snap and pop beneath my boots, imagining that each step is imprinting itself on the ground, that each moment is making its mark on me with the ink of my own attention.

INVITATION FOR WRITING & REFLECTION

Try walking meditation in your house or out in the yard, even if you feel self-conscious about it at first. For ten minutes, feel every flex of the muscles in your legs as your feet press against the earth like a seal. Keep your focus on all the sensations in your body, and then afterward, sit down and write for fifteen minutes about those moments. How did it feel to walk with so much care? Did your mind slow down as you slowed your steps?

Meditation Class

I paused in the rain outside the storefront,
though there was no sign, only the image
of a lotus on the steamed-over window.
Inside, rows of people crouched on cushions,
eyes closed, their legs folded beneath them.
Some were mouthing what I took to be
a mantra, a few words in Sanskrit meant
to make them hum as one with the universe.
I wiped the fog from the glass and saw
a statue of the Buddha on a shelf, laughing
at himself, laughing at me standing there
in a puddle, under a pine tree that kept
dripping on my head, keeping perfect time
with my heartbeat. The night seemed to slow
the longer I watched those students going
nowhere and doing nothing together—
until there were no more worries about
the rent, no sick parents or ex-boyfriends.
Only a car passing by on the slick street,
the sound of something being torn in two.

I had just begun a daily meditation practice when I came upon this scene in the city, walking home from the bus stop.

The class was taking place in a yoga studio, and I had often seen the people inside twisted into complex positions when I passed by before. But I had never seen them "doing nothing and going nowhere" together like this, each person crouched on a cushion and emanating positivity, presence, and a deep and abiding joy. This moment changed me as I watched those people meditating as one group, one "sangha," as Buddhists often call communities of practitioners. I knew as soon as I saw them: *I want that kind of peace.*

Yet it has been a struggle for me to establish my own meditation and prayer practice. I try to set aside at least twenty minutes each morning to sit and simply be, yet it is seldom pleasant or comfortable, and it's difficult to remember that it's not really supposed to be. We meditate to make space in our lives, hearts, and minds for whatever comes up. It can be discouraging, however, to realize just how jumpy our thoughts can be. Eventually, though, after years of reading books, attending retreats, and above all, continually trying on my own, I felt like one of those people I saw years ago, crouched on their cushions with eyes closed and legs twisted beneath them. My own years of practice have taught me that there is no right or wrong way to meditate, just as there is no right or wrong way to write. We have to find what works for us.

As in life, we experiment in playful, loose ways, and trust that what we are drawn to will always offer us what we need. This is as true in meditation as it is in my writing practice; if I can, I simply let the movements of my mind guide me, unfolding on their own on the page. If nothing else, mindfulness has taught me to pay deeper attention to my own body and the emotions that pass through, as well as to my own senses, the way the sound of a car passing by on a slick street can still take me out of my head and ground me in the now. The way a simple moment—seeing a group of people sitting still in a yoga studio, for instance—can follow me for the rest of my life.

INVITATION FOR WRITING & REFLECTION

Write about a time when you observed someone who seemed peaceful or happy, when you perhaps felt envious because you wanted the same feeling of peace. How did witnessing such peace in another person cause a shift in your own life and mind?

Fireflies

We are like someone in a very dark night over whom lightning flashes again and again.

—**Maimonides**

Some insights come like lightning—
blinding and fierce—while others arrive
as firefly-flashes that brighten only
an inch or so of air around them.
Yet even these can gather power,
if given time, like the summer night
I woke and stood at the window
to watch all that pulsing outside—
like thousands of prayers flaring up
above the houses, saying *here*
and *here* and *here* as I made my way
down the stairs using only the light
of those small bodies to guide me.

We might expect that we will someday reach a place where only the light of joy and understanding graces our lives.

Yet it seems we get only flashes of insight, off and on, to guide us into our depths. As the 12th-century rabbi and philosopher Maimonides pointed out: The trick is both to notice and appreciate those lightning-fast flashes of clarity when they come in the midst of darkness, sometimes staying for only a second or two.

One morning, I rose before first light, unable to sleep, and flashed on this truth: Our insights often feel dimmer and more brief, even than lightning, because they originate out of the ordinariness of daily life. We have mistakenly trained ourselves to look for and remember only the larger-than-life moments, instead of those smaller and more commonplace instances of awakening to the actual. Yet, if we keep looking past the so-called small things, discounting such moments because we believe that enlightenment will arrive as one prolonged period of blindingly bright revelation, then we may be even less present for the next moment of presence, and the next. Any brief and bright thing can bring us closer to our spiritual and creative selves—whether stopping to admire fireflies outside, with their instinctive flares like prayers for visibility, or feeling warm air scented with Queen Anne's lace wafting through the window screen. We can never predict what will awaken us to the life we're meant to live.

INVITATION FOR WRITING & REFLECTION

Consider a time when an unexpected realization, no matter how brief or dim, entered your life. Describe how it changed you, even if for just a few minutes. Did it feel like lightning, swift and fierce, or was the light more subtle than that?

Note to Self

Leave the TV off tonight and put
your phone on silent. Pour the wine
in your glass down the drain.
Taste the homemade raspberry jam
friends sent packed in a box
with balled-up newspaper so the jar
wouldn't break on its way to you.
Treat each fragile moment like that
and make of this instant something
sweet to smear on toasted bread,
then feast alone while standing
and staring out at the bare magnolia.

I once lived in a house with a massive magnolia in the backyard.

It was always an event when its gaudy pink blossoms finally eased open, fallen petals softening the brick walkway from the garage to the back door for weeks. Yet, I admit, I did not always stop to appreciate that tree as much as I would have liked, and there were times when life felt so overwhelming, I did not notice it was blooming until long after this had begun to happen.

I wrote this poem one evening when I felt especially restless, unable to come down from the busyness of the work week. I paced the house, finishing chores then bouncing like a pinball from one distraction to the next, looking for something, anything, to help calm me. I poured a tall glass of red wine, turned on the TV, texted friends—but none of my usual escapes were working. Finally, I realized that I'd been looking for an answer outside of myself, when the solution would come, as always, from within. All I really needed to do was get still and let the rushed energy left over from the week fully leave my body. I poured the rest of the wine down the drain, turned off the TV, and put my phone on silent so I would stop obsessively checking it.

I sat at my kitchen table for a long time, and slowly began to appreciate the small miracles that were right in front of me— the jar of raspberry jam friends had shipped from Minnesota, the buttery toast I made with it, and the magnolia whose twisted limbs seemed so alive to me, even in the bareness of winter. During those few minutes alone at the table, doing nothing, I let the unadorned beauty of my life as it was, and not as it could be or should be, seep back into my weary bones. I felt just like that magnolia, soaking up the last light of the day and storing it for the moment it would break into blossom again.

INVITATION FOR WRITING & REFLECTION

What are some of the ways you use to escape when you feel especially restless? When you sit still, peeling back the anxious energy so many of us now live with, what do you notice that is worthy of appreciation? What are some of those everyday miracles that appear right in front of you?

How to Meet a Moment

To embrace a moment fully,
surrender your thoughts to the grass
between your toes, let droplets
of dew kiss your bare feet
with innocence, like children.

Walk the path to the apple tree
planted a hundred years ago,
now supporting the graft of a few
leafed-out branches that hold
the sunshine like a basket.

Hold sorrow too, let it rise in you
like yeasty sourdough left alone
in a warm place on the table,
and relish this necessary grief,
the bread of which also feeds you.

But once you're finished feeling it,
be done. Find some other wondrous
thing to give your whole self to—
blue twine woven in a warbler's nest,
the seedheads of rye grass waving
in wind, the blades suddenly parting
like the sea for you to enter.

When we can surrender our thoughts and expectations for how things will turn out, we allow ourselves to sink deeply into the present like a bare foot in wet grass, feeling the lushness, softness, and chill of each blade.

Once we find a space of time stretching out before us, a certain amount of unfelt sadness from the past might arise alongside the joy, might even expand in us like dough rising on its own. When this happens to me, I sometimes panic and want to close down what I see as a negative feeling. I can be sitting out in the yard, having a quiet afternoon, when thoughts of my brother, who hasn't spoken to me in years, suddenly sweep in, when worries about his well-being and what I might have done to hurt him take over my mind. The question then becomes: What do I do with those feelings? Do I pull out my phone, reach for something that pushes those thoughts away for a brief time?

If I aim to be there fully, I have to be present to the pleasure and the pain, which always coexist. One is not better than the other, though we often tell ourselves that pain is a punishment for what we've done wrong, and pleasure a reward for what's right in our lives. Thoughts like this—and they are just thoughts—lift us out of the moment and put up barriers between the self and what we are really feeling.

A thought will sometimes take us away for a while. A hidden grief will call to us. Yet we can make it a practice to feel it all, and then be done with it, let it pass through us as it will, pouring out onto the page. We can rejoice in the fact that we are alive enough to feel it in the first place, because whatever we try to numb also weakens the joyful, playful, creative spirit in us as well. Holding all of it at once, we may feel as battered as an ancient apple tree, yet see the miracle of those new branches grafted to its trunk, how they form a kind of basket that holds the light that feeds them. See how a field of waving rye grass can beckon you back to yourself, parting its blue-green blades for you to enter this moment with gratitude for whatever arises in you.

INVITATION FOR WRITING & REFLECTION

What does it feel like for you to enter a moment fully, holding everything you feel at the same time? You might begin with the phrase, "To enter a moment fully . . ." and see what instructions come to you.

PART FIVE

Poems for Gratefulness and Joy

What brings fulfillment is gratefulness,
the simple response of our heart to this
given life in all its fullness.

—Brother David Steindl-Rast

Here with You

It's too hot on this summer afternoon
to move from our places on the couch,
even to slice the peach still waiting
on the counter for the kiss of the knife.

A different kind of hunger keeps me
here with you, rubbing the fine hairs
on your arms that have turned blond
after all those hours in the sun,

and which are just now catching
the light, spinning it into gold I want
to touch over and over, never once
having dreamed I'd ever be this rich.

Feelings of true wealth and abundance come in those moments we realize the value of what we already have.

Often, it takes some outer stress to bring us to this place of greater gratitude and presence. Perhaps a health scare or harrowing transition help us see how easily our world can shatter and shift around us. We might then appreciate the sudden blessing, for instance, of sitting on the couch with a loved one on an unbearably hot summer day, knowing that nothing else needs to be done, and the feast of a ripe peach waits on the counter. I wrote this poem weeks after my husband and I had come down with COVID-19. Brad's illness lasted so long that he ended up in the ER several times with symptoms no doctor could explain. For a while, we wondered if he would ever get better, but then slowly, the vertigo and nausea began to lift, and he was able to go back to work.

Life returned to normal for us, though I felt anything but. I had been transformed by his brush with mortality, and the way the shadow of illness hung over all we did for a month. Once the darkness of that time faded, I couldn't help but feel more grateful for ordinary evenings together, just sitting beside him and touching those blond hairs on his arms as if they were actual gold. We don't want to dress-rehearse tragedy, or live in such fear of death that we end up paralyzed, unable to thrive. Yet, we can walk with the knowledge that change is the nature of every life on this planet, allowing our awareness to turn everyday moments into experiences we will relish and remember forever. When we pause in the middle of our rushed and worry-filled lives to say even a silent thank you, we drop more deeply into ourselves, into the current of life. The richness may not last forever, but the more we practice both gratitude and joy—in our lives and in our creativity—the more we will build the habit of finding abundance right in front of us.

INVITATION FOR WRITING & REFLECTION

Have you had a moment like this, perhaps after a trying or frightening period, when love and abundance came together and left you feeling more grateful than ever for the blessing of simple things?

Early Spring Prayer

You can't endure a winter like this
without wanting to kneel and kiss
the green blades of each daffodil
reaching up through leftover snow.
But you don't have to scrape your knees
or fold both hands in order to pray.
The way you shed your coat today
and angle your face up toward the sun
is enough to say please and thank you
over and over, feeling yourself
soften along with the earth, some
part of you reclaiming its color
like the goldfinch whose yellow
feathers are just beginning to show
as he cracks open the seed of this day.

Some of us might feel put off by the word "prayer" because of negative experiences with organized religion or the belief that the act of prayer must unfold in a certain way.

Yet, as I say in this poem, we might widen our definition of what it means to pray to include gratefulness for a warm day in spring, for instance, or the sudden relief of seeing the blades of daffodils at last reaching up through thawing soil. Prayer for me has little to do with whether or not we fold our hands and get down on our knees, and it is not necessarily a specific plea we make to our version of the Creator. Instead, I see prayer as an opening to the world, a shedding of our coats—and perhaps the armor we sometimes put on as a way to make ourselves less vulnerable to disappointment and pain. Prayer is more of a softening, like the earth each spring, which allows both beauty and pain to move through us, and lets the roots of who we are seek out what they need to feel nourished.

The day that inspired this poem remains a vivid one for me, as the heaviness and dullness of that winter began to lift, and I felt myself reclaiming a joy that had always been there, just waiting beneath the surface. Yet, I would never have been able to write this, or feel the utter freedom of that early spring day, if I had not given myself permission to take the time, drive to town, and just walk around in the sunshine without a coat for a while. I was resistant, of course, as I often am to tending my own delight, but the reward was this awakening into a space of gratitude for even the slightest signs that the season was finally shifting. We all know the feeling of angling our faces up to a warmer sun and the helpless "thank you" we say under our breath for the light and heat. As the German theologian Meister Eckhart once wrote: "If the only prayer you ever say in your entire life is thank you, it will be enough." Perhaps we can take the pressure off ourselves to pray in a specific way, and trust that it is enough to say "please" and "thank you," to take pleasure in the seed of each new day offered to us, and crack it open like the feast it is.

INVITATION FOR WRITING & REFLECTION

Widening your own definition of what it means to pray, describe a time when you stayed open to the world around you and felt a sense of gratitude. What brings you relief and joy in your surroundings right now, and how might you allow yourself to "shed your coat," receiving it all more deeply? Write your own prayer of gratefulness that you might return to during difficult times.

Praise Song

And when the world refuses,
you must sing your own praises,
must let that music rise up
from the deepest places in you
and pour out its shameless hymn.
Listen to water as it seeps
between gaps in rocks, how
the Rottweiler next door looses
a string of barks and snarls, warning
anyone who passes by to think
twice before entering his yard.
Hear the hum of the fridge chilling
the milk, the butter, the sweating
pitcher of lemonade, how everything
sings of itself, even the coffeemaker
flipped on with a careless touch
this morning, puffing and croaking
its own wisdom like the chorus
of peepers who have come again
to the creek this spring, who spend
all day and night praising
the mud they slip deeper into,
singing of the warmth that fills them.

When I stand at the edge of Warm Brook, by the old stone wall near our house, and listen to the spring peepers filling the night with a song that belongs only to them, I am brought back to the moment and the physicality of my own body.

I become a participant in their singing, and attune myself to all the sounds of this planet, to the way objects and living beings alike all sing of themselves without shame or fear. I often consider how they invite us to do the same, to let our own shameless hymns pour forth, especially at those times when we feel the world is a difficult and unwelcoming place.

Listening, though, is just one of the many ways we can ground ourselves and leave behind the distracting streams of thought that keep us from noticing and receiving so much. If we allow them, all the senses will help us enter our lives more fully, even the Rottweiler next door whose barks and snarls we can hardly stand. He, too, reminds me of my aliveness, if I can learn to praise whatever awakens me—the puff and croak of the coffeemaker, the humming fridge—and know that the world always offers itself, waiting for the praise that makes us pay even closer attention. When we learn to praise the presence of even the simplest things in our lives, we access a deeper music that lives inside us all, and live from that grateful place no matter what else happens, no matter our annoyance or anger, our persistent wish for things to be other than they are. In other words, we find our joy, which is, as the Benedictine monk Brother David Steindl-Rast reminds us, "the happiness that doesn't depend on what happens."

INVITATION FOR WRITING & REFLECTION

Begin with a specific sensory experience (of taste, sight, smell, sound, or touch), and see where that leads you. You might explore all the various, interconnected ways that sense invites us back into the body and can make a paradise of the moment at hand. You might also try praising all the things you feel grateful for in your surroundings right now.

Counting Blessings

I'm stringing together my gratitudes
like these unruly preschoolers I see
crossing the street in a snaking line,
tethered to each other by a strong
neon-green rope, protected from traffic
as they shout and strain to break away.
I count my blessings to keep them close:
this body, this house, this one heart
creaking open to let in the spring sun
as I say thank you to the black-capped
flashes of chickadees at the feeder,
to sudden sleet, and stones half-buried
in our yard, having melted the snow
from around their mossy skin, each one
now somehow warmer to the touch.

"Count your blessings" is one of those bits of age-old wisdom that might sound quaint and out of touch to our modern ears.

Yet, once we actually put the words into practice and feel the results, we understand why even scientists now cite the tangible benefits of cultivating gratitude each day, blessing those *specific* aspects of life that give us pleasure in the moment. This is why I believe I gravitate so much toward the practice of writing poetry, which invites specificity, which pulls me so often back into my senses where true presence begins. It might be the slants of stronger spring light falling across the wall, or the black-capped chickadee whose playful flitting calls us back to the act of gratitude. Whatever it is, I do my best to say "thank you" over and over, even if I can't quite let go of what's bothering me at first.

I started this poem while writing in my journal during a difficult time with a co-worker, when anger and frustration had become constant companions in my body, and I felt betrayed by his actions. Yet, I knew that if I didn't do *something* to shift my thinking, I would keep focusing on all the perceived wrongs, instead of generating warmth and thanks for all that was going well in my life, and for all that we had also taught each other. This is how the process of gratefulness works for me: I begin by stringing together those specific blessings that first come to mind, then adding more and more, like beads on a necklace or that string of preschoolers, even when my mind wants to break away. We often crave the seeming solidity of negativity, some problem to grasp and hold onto, especially when we find ourselves in uncertain times or feel especially vulnerable. And we can keep generating that dark, sticky energy, which feels so seductive at times.

If we let the process of gratitude take hold, however, we might be led toward a sudden appreciation for this one life, for the privilege of aliveness that includes the sorrows and joys, angers and fears, all at the same time. We can also move from a more general gratitude into the smaller, specific delights we uncover as we do our best to release negative thoughts. In my case, it was the chickadees, pellets of sleet careening down, and those stones in our yard whose subtle warmth melts the snow piled on top of them very slowly, leaving a hollow bowl all around. I came upon the rocks during a walk that morning, and though I had noticed this phenomenon before, I never really thought about how it must be warmer underground, even if only slightly, and how this warmth waits just beneath the surface in each of us, too, if we are willing to pause and praise this world, just as it is.

INVITATION FOR WRITING & REFLECTION

What does it feel like to count your blessings? What images arise in your mind as you cultivate your own joy in specific things? You might allow a list to form, using the phrase, "I say "thank you" to . . ." over and over, then filling in the blanks.

Down to Earth

The heart of a farmer
is made of muscle
and earth that aches
for return to earth.
And when the sky
releases a steady rain,
massaging each row
of sprouted beans,
my husband leans out
of the car window
and opens his hand
to hold that water
for a single instant,
his heart now beating
in sync with rain
seeping through layers
to kiss the roots
of every plant alive
on this living, breathing
planet on whose back
we were granted
permission to live
for a limited time.

We tend to believe that our power comes from the accumulation of outer status, achievements, and material things.

Yet, real power comes from within and emanates from a heart filled with gratitude for the life we have. My husband, who's worked as an organic farmer for more than a decade, has taught me over the years to "lead with love," as he often says, and to live from the space of the heart, letting intuition guide my actions. This has not been an easy journey for someone who spent most of his life trapped in fantasy or planning several steps ahead so as to avoid pain and discomfort. As a teacher, I also once placed a premium on living from the head, from analysis and so-called reason, believing I could create formulas to predict and control the future.

Yet, living from the heart seems a more organic practice, allowing us to connect more deeply not only with ourselves and each other, but also with the natural world. After spending a few hours among the trees or in an overgrown field, without distraction, just absorbing everything that happens, it's hard not to feel a sense of awe for this "living, breathing planet." The central image of this poem for me, though, is my husband's open hand, because it is precisely this kind of receptivity to the world that helps us live more connected, wholehearted lives. And perhaps we awaken gratefulness the most when we remember how limited our time might be.

INVITATION FOR WRITING & REFLECTION

You might begin by writing about someone you love, or even exploring the nature of your own heart. Try starting with the phrase, "The heart is made of . . ." letting that lead you into the writing.

When I Can Do Nothing Else Today

Let me pause in the softening field
like a bed stripped bare of its sheet
and find spinach still growing there
in neat rows after months of snow.
Let me pick a few of the new leaves
and feast on them with sun slanting
welcome in my winter eyes, exciting
my skin to shivers. And let me savor
the sweetness of meager spring light
already turned to sugar in this green
I chew along with a few grains of sand
that remind me there is only so much
time to kneel and pray like this.

In spite of months of brutal cold and snow, it always seems a miracle to me that things return, struggling back up from the once-frozen earth.

Such was the case with the rows of spinach I found growing again one morning as I walked the farm fields around our house. As I knelt in the softening soil, I saw the dark green leaves uncurling again, absorbing what light they could. It felt like a sudden promise that I might do the same. Sometimes, when we have lost faith, lost heart, lost hope that our circumstances will change, the world gives us just enough of what we need to keep growing ourselves. And when we allow even the slightest internal shift, even the plainest moments can become more precious to us.

Perhaps one gateway to gratitude is learning to "love our likes" once more, embracing those things we simply enjoy as a necessary part of our daily routine, like a prescription we write for ourselves. That might mean making time for writing, getting together with friends for coffee, or visiting a favorite restaurant more frequently. And if we start to feel that we are being too "self-indulgent," we can simply say: This is my medicine, this is what I need. Once I discovered that spinach growing in the field, for weeks I made it a daily practice to come and visit it, now and then eating a few of the surprisingly sweet leaves. We think we have to take larger action and make grander gestures, yet on the most difficult days, this is what saves us—cultivating the small joys that call to us and reclaiming the world's resilience as our own.

INVITATION FOR WRITING & REFLECTION

What causes you to stop and remember that there will be only so much time to appreciate this world? Begin with the phrase, "Let me pause . . ." and see what springs to mind.

Sunflower

"Joy is not made to be a crumb,"
Mary Oliver once wrote, but isn't that
how it often shows up at first? One crumb
of attention, then another, and another
until you're able to follow the trail
leading to the volunteer sunflower
you hadn't noticed blooming by the garden.
"Volunteer," we say, meaning no human
hand nestled that seed in the ground,
though the same could be said of joy too,
which seems to spring up out of nowhere
when you see the face of the flower
the French call *tournesol*, meaning
"turned toward the sun." And don't we
each carry a small sun in our chests
that tells us where to turn, where it's warm,
where something bright has struggled up
out of the earth, and is now calling our name?

Joy begins when we pay attention to the world both outside of and within us.

Little by little, as we give ourselves over to what calls our name, as we surrender to it, we find a sudden warmth flooding our chests like a small sun nudging us toward the light. Then we can't help but turn toward what brings that feeling again and again, even if we don't fully understand it at first. How could a knee-high volunteer sunflower possibly offer me so much joy that I was moved to sit down and write an entire poem about it? How could something so ordinary, having likely sprung up from a seed some squirrel buried in the yard before winter, spark such reverence and wonder? I can't quite say, of course, because joys both large and small resist being pinned down by words and our human desire for explanation. The simplest answer is: Joy is joy, and we can choose to embrace it when it comes, or turn away.

Like so many of my poems, this one arose out of a time of struggle when my mother was ill, and I realized that I'd been overworking myself so as not to face that fact, or feel the deep grief that came intertwined with it. The gardens that Brad had planted all around our yard became a refuge for me, and I made it a practice to spend at least a few hours each day weeding, watering, and wandering among the lush beauty of black-eyed Susans, helianthus, echinacea, and so much more.

All that summer, I wanted to escape the truth that my mother was dying, and I often spent long hours working in front of screens, losing myself in novels whose plots I barely remember now. Yet, I found that, as so many wise teachers tell us, you can't numb one emotion without numbing them all. By pushing down the grief and fear of losing my mother, I also cut myself off from the joy that springs up out of nowhere. Because joy happens so spontaneously, it needs space and presence to move through us. These trips out into the yard brought me back to nature and the life I no longer wanted to deny. And one morning, while tipping the watering can toward a clump of native grasses, I saw the yellow face of a sunflower that had struggled up to claim its place on the earth. The leaves were curled and slightly eaten, and it seemed to have trouble peering above the grasses surrounding it. But there was no denying that wild brightness, or the flame of joy it lit in me.

We lose ourselves by pushing down thoughts and emotions, yet moments like this show us it doesn't have to stay that way. Perhaps the power of any writing practice is that we become able, over time, to recognize the instant we come back to our lives, when we are paying enough attention to what calls our name. This is what we mean by presence, which is the gateway toward any of the positive emotions we hope to cultivate for wholeness—kindness, gratitude, mindfulness, or joy. If we can be fully present to the thrill of finding a volunteer sunflower blooming by the garden, perhaps we can also give space to all that wants to bloom in us, too, throwing the heart open to a world that will cause us suffering, yes, but which also offers the chance for healing in countless ways each day.

INVITATION FOR WRITING & REFLECTION

Describe in specific detail some small joy that called you out of numbness and back to the life at hand. How did that joy feel as it arose in you? You might also jump off from the quote by Mary Oliver that begins my poem, "Joy is not made to be a crumb," seeing where her wise words lead you.

Evening Light

There is this place on the table
next to the couch where light
always rests at sunset, reaching
through the leaves of the cherry tree
to touch the keychain and calendar,
the wallet and change, one last time
before night falls. That would make
a great photo, I think, ready to reach
for my phone, move the vase of cut
sunflowers closer, so they too might
blaze up and burn. Instead, I stay
right where I am, deciding to leave
the moment intact, tinged orange
with smoke from wildfires up north,
the whole house now held in the
amber of that dying light.

I often write to preserve some bit of aliveness,
so that I may return to the same sense of
vitality later on.

Of course, the goal is to lead our lives so that we are actually here to receive the moments that matter, which often show up in the slightest, most surprising ways. This poem was born one evening after Brad and I had finished eating supper, and I was cleaning up the dishes. I looked over, as I often do, at that place on the side table where I'd noticed light rests as the sun begins to set outside. There it was again, shining through the leaves of the cherry tree, filling our whole living room before nightfall. I felt a sensation of warmth filling me too, a wholeness that had been missing for a while. "Is this joy?" I thought, and knew that it was, fleeting though it might be.

In his essay, "On Little Joys," the novelist and Nobel Prize winner Herman Hesse says, "I believe what we lack is joy. The ardor that a heightened awareness imparts to life, the conception of life as a happy thing, as a festival . . . but the high value put upon every minute of time." I love the idea of treating each moment of life like a festival, of offering a heightened awareness to every instant that we can. Why should a simple patch of light shining on a side table bring me such pleasure? I can only say it is the awareness that arises when we decide not to disrupt our moments with devices, with intrusive thoughts or worries, when we leave the moment intact, even if it's tinged with grief and fear brought about by the smoke of wildfires raging just to the north. Joy and ardor are still here, too, waiting inside the small, personal things that we notice, which bring us home to ourselves.

INVITATION FOR WRITING & REFLECTION

Describe a moment that you left intact for yourself, deciding not to disrupt it. Is there some unsnapped photo or video that still stays with you, even though you refused to document the moment of attention until now? Bring the reader into every detail of that little joy as you re-create it. You might begin by saying, "I went to reach for my phone, but . . ." and see what arises from there.

World Prayer Day

While people all over the world
chanted and prayed for a miracle,
we stood in the woods with binoculars
trained on a pair of bluebirds
flitting from branch to branch,
their tiny chests puffed out
in the chill morning air. And for those
few moments, mud frozen
beneath our feet and not a single
golden leaf stirring on the beech tree,
I did not think about a virus entering
my body after turning a doorknob
or shaking someone's hand or breathing
their breath. It was as if those two
bluebirds became parts of us freed
at last from worry—our tufted, lighter
bodies now lifting higher and higher,
like words meant for whatever god
must still be listening.

This poem arrived at the height of the COVID pandemic on a day when friends had sent me messages that people were gathering at a particular time to chant and pray for some miraculous breakthrough to end the world's suffering.

Later, as my husband and I hiked through the woods near our house, I realized that as we stood there focused on a male and female pair of bluebirds, we were enacting our own form of prayer. When Brad passed me the binoculars, and I saw the startling blue coats of those birds up close, their downy chests the color of vellum, it dawned on me that we were allowing the natural world to lift us out of our fearful, uncertain minds and into a space beyond worry for our safety and the health of our loved ones. Just standing there, giving the blessing of our attention to something outside ourselves, we became lighter, and I began to feel some of the first glimmers of hope that we might endure this dark and difficult time in all of our lives.

The sight of those bluebirds taught me a few essential lessons. The first is that when we can't engage in our own self-care, when we can't lift ourselves out of despair, sometimes the world will do it for us, taking care of our needs almost without our knowing it. But we must engage with the world, placing ourselves in the path of joy and doing the things that inspire us, even if we don't feel the positive effects right away. I had planned to take part in the worldwide prayer circle happening that day, but when the shy March sun came out, I found that I couldn't resist some time outside in the woods. The longer we spent among the trees, the more I knew that this too was a form of prayer for me. Perhaps I did not need to sit on a meditation cushion to show my reverence and care for the living beings all around me. Maybe one of the most potent prayers for the world is to interact with beeches and bluebirds, feeling the ridges of frozen mud beneath our boots. Whatever grounds us in the moment, after all, is bound to make us better humans. What if we let our joy become a wish for the well-being of everyone, that we all might be lifted out of our smaller selves and into a deeper communion?

INVITATION FOR WRITING & REFLECTION

What does it mean for you to place yourself in the path of joy? You might describe a time when a sudden flash of delight allowed you to move past your own busyness or grief into a place of greater lightness and beauty.

Necessary Beauty

Though we had suitcases to pack
and bags of dog food to haul home,
it was necessary for us to drive instead
toward the arboretum, where lilacs
at last in bloom filled the evening air
with their perfume. It was necessary
to get out of the car, kick off our shoes
and walk barefoot onto the steaming,
sun-warmed mulch among the bushes,
to take a blossom-heavy branch
in each hand and inhale deeply so we
could breathe again after the longest
winter in memory. It was necessary
to close our eyes and sigh, to see
what had been driving the bees so wild
all day, making them dance above us
as we collapsed in the dewy grass,
half-high on that commonplace scent
of spring we'd find hours later, clinging
to our shirts, our skin, our hair.

My friend Heather and I were driving home from the grocery store in rush hour traffic that April day.

There were still dishes to do from our dinner party last night, and each of us had hours of work to finish. Yet, our rolled-down windows told us it was spring at last, the air soft and warm and flooded with light. Suddenly, Heather turned to me. "Should we stop at the arboretum?" she asked. "Do we have time?" I hesitated, looking at the clock, but luckily, she didn't wait for my answer. She made a U-turn and drove there anyway. "We have to go," she said. "The lilacs are finally in bloom."

When we got out of the car, both of us kicked off our sandals so we could step barefoot through sun-struck grass, among the trees, to the grove of lilacs. Bees danced and buzzed in the air around us. I couldn't stop bringing each purple, blossom-heavy branch close to my face and inhaling as if that scent were a medicine I had needed all winter without realizing it. "See," Heather said, "there's always time for lilacs."

In the end, she was right, and as poet and essayist Robert Bly has pointed out, "We are like poor students who stay after school to study joy." We don't believe that joy can be one of the reasons we're here on earth, or we try to make a formula of it, breaking it down into theories and ideas, instead of simply experiencing the pleasure when it arrives. Why should joy not be a part of our common core curriculum, at least as important as chemistry and long division? We are born with access to joy and live in a world still filled with countless reasons to rejoice. Yet, we need to be reminded it exists these days when we spend so much of our time in front of screens or working to acquire and achieve, often at the expense of spontaneity and play. We must each make a living or go to school, it's true, but let's not put off our joy until the end of the week or the start of our next vacation. Let's not put off doing what we love until we retire at the end of our lives. Let's find small ways to feel it in the here and now, as my friend and I did that day, taking a twenty-minute detour to smell those flowers that marked the end of a long and lightless winter. Let's be students of the joy that's available each time we decide to seize it for ourselves.

INVITATION FOR WRITING & REFLECTION

Describe a time when you swept aside your obligations and tasks for the day to follow your joy instead. Were you able to feel the uplift fully, or were you still checking your phone, thinking about what needed to be done? You might also write about what you would do if someone gave you permission right now to take an hour just for yourself and pursue something that deeply calls to you.

PART SIX

Poems for Wonder and Awe

*Human beings must always be on the
watch for the coming of wonders.*

—E. B. White

Awe

It's a shiver that climbs the trellis
of the spine, each tingle a bright
white morning glory bursting into blossom
beneath the skin. It can happen anywhere,
anytime, even finding a sleeve of ice
worn by a branch all morning, now fallen
on a bed of snow. You can choose to pause,
pick it up, hold that cold thing in your hand
or not. Few tell us that wonder and awe
are decisions we make daily, hourly,
minute by minute in the tiny offices
of the heart, tilting the head to look up
at every tree turned into a chandelier
by light striking ice in just the right way.

We forget that awe is a choice we can make for ourselves from moment to moment in daily life.

Yet mindfulness and the regular cultivation of attention can show us that we need not wait for wonder and inspiration to find us—we can go seeking it on our own, listening for the whispers that want us to pause and take in some small but no less marvelous thing. Though there are plenty of times when I ignore these whispers, I was luckily receptive on the day I describe here, trudging through snow on a trail near my house, caught in the loop of my own thoughts until I noticed that cast-off sleeve of ice resting beneath a tree. We'd had a wild ice storm the night before, and I'd seen the cold gleam of bare branches now encased all around me. But this sleeve of ice—just a little glimmer in the corner of my eye—caught my attention and made me stop to pick it up, hold it in my hand, touch the bits of lichen that must have peeled away from the branch when the ice gave way.

We often stop for the new, for things we've never seen before. But there is a case to be made for turning fresh eyes on what we think of as the ordinary stuff because, as poet Jacqueline Suskin has pointed out in Every Day Is a Poem, we never know when we'll be seeing things for the very last time. As she writes: "The fact that it could all be gone at any moment, that all of our experience is tangled up with so much pain and loss, is part of why it's so amazing to rejoice in every offering that life throws our way." When we feel the push to move past what's calling us to pause and marvel, maybe we can remember that those whispers of awe are here to bring us relief, to open up space, even when we're struggling. And when we do listen, we often become available for even more moments of wonder, as when I glanced up at the icy trees and found the thin winter sunlight had transformed them into chandeliers, shining—or so it seemed in that instant—just for me.

INVITATION FOR WRITING & REFLECTION

As you move through the next few days, see if you can be available for simple moments of wonder that call to you. How does the sensation of awe feel in the body, and what brought it about? You could write the phrase "Awe is . . ." at the top of the page, and list what springs to mind.

After the Blizzard

You might be without power, sipping
cold coffee in the dark, with only
an orange to eat. But don't the trees
each glow in their sleeves of heavy snow,
don't you live inside a cathedral
of white limbs reaching upward, with flakes
still gathering around you like the world's
finally paying attention?

Let your thoughts,
wishes, and obligations all fall away
like the peels of this orange, revealing
every sweet section beneath. Believe
that awe will follow you from now on
wherever you go, like the snow-light
that fills these rooms, like the scent of citrus,
which passes from your hands to every
small thing you touch.

Wonder and awe don't always come to us on their own.

Often, we must choose to cultivate what best-selling author Katherine May calls "enchantment" with our daily surroundings, even—and perhaps especially—during times of strife. As she writes in Enchantment: "If we start to re-enchant the most fundamental parts of our existence—the food, the objects we use, the places we inhabit—we can begin to restore our connection between our bodies and the land." This poem arrived for me during a power outage when I felt disenchanted and helpless to be without electricity, unable to open the refrigerator, use the faucets, or take a shower for days. Everything felt more complicated and difficult, but when I let myself pause with a cup of cold coffee, I saw the privilege of my own fortunate life. I looked out the window and noticed the unmistakable beauty of wet snow clinging to the bare branches of every tree, the pines bent over and drooping under the weight of their fluffy white coats. I didn't feel grateful for all the trouble the two feet of snow was causing my husband and me, or the danger it surely imposed on others. But taking the time to awaken wonder made me realize that, as with so much in life, how I react to my present circumstances is largely a choice. Yes, I might feel vulnerable, living without power for several days. But I could also decide to open to the awe literally pressing against my windows.

Perhaps my restlessness and inability to appreciate the deep pause of this storm also meant that I desperately needed the rest I kept resisting. Sometimes, when we crave stillness the most, we push against it, not wanting to disrupt the momentum of the busy and frantic energy that infects us. Yet, more often than not, when I choose to meditate, take a slow walk, or simply look out the window with a quiet sense of reverence for the power of nature, I reach a place of greater surrender. A tiny door opens in the heart, and inspiration filters in like the snow-light that filled every room in the house. When we notice and nourish this fuller presence in the world, it infuses each moment for hours after, like the scent of an orange that clings to our fingers and rubs off on every small thing we touch.

INVITATION FOR WRITING & REFLECTION

Write about a time when you felt worried or fearful, and were lifted out of the emotion by the physical world. See if you can capture the flavor of your sudden relief using specific details from your experience. Moving forward, how might you cultivate more ordinary awe in daily life?

Sea Glass

We keep going back to the rocky beach,
searching for the glint of sea glass—
the white, the green, the rarest blue.
It takes decades to smooth out the sharp
edges of those shards, years of helpless
turning in the tides, so we might then
reach down, slip one into our pocket
and run fingers over the worn surface
when worry takes over a quiet mind.
We too have been tumbled by the waves
of life, and with each passing year, I feel
my own edges buffed and polished so I
might slide more easily through the hours,
stop resisting the pull of whatever ocean
I'm in. Once, I wanted to be the shimmering
bottle, container to hold the whole world
impossibly inside myself, but now I just want
to be the piece of beauty you come upon
in an otherwise calm moment, cradled
by the endless sea crashing at your feet.

My husband and I are hopeless beachcombers.

Each time we vacation near the ocean, we end up kneeling in sand or rocks, digging and digging until we've amassed a pile of shells, pottery shards, and sea glass. It doesn't matter that the jars and bowls of our treasure sit scattered around the house, gathering dust. We hunt and gather without a purpose, as a practice of mindfulness and play. The thrill comes in finding the sea glass especially, watching for the telltale glint as we walk. I think we enjoy the search so much because it causes us to pay attention to our surroundings in a way that we normally wouldn't, which is, of course, the source of all wonder and awe. When caught in fear or worry, the most reliable cure I know is to focus outward, to lose myself in some physical, tangible act of attention. As Robin Wall Kimmerer has written: "Attention is the doorway to gratitude, the doorway to wonder, the doorway to reciprocity." By focusing on the world around us, we give back to the world, and, in the process, to ourselves.

I keep pieces of sea glass in my pocket for this very reason, especially if I know I'm going to be in a situation that causes anxiety. When I feel my heart leaping and heat spreading through my chest, I can reach down, run a finger along those buffed and polished edges. My whole nervous system calms down. Sea glass also reminds me of all the ways I've been smoothed by the pull of whatever ocean I'm in, by the helpless passage of time. Holding a piece of it in my palm, I feel awe at how I've grown softer over the years with myself and others, able to send more compassion inward and outward, too. Having written seriously for several decades now, my ambition has shifted from wanting to absorb and hold the entirety of the world inside myself to simply staying awake to the wonder of how things are. My only hope as both writer and human is to be a part of something much larger than myself. Let the waves toss me, if they must. But let me also trust that I will be carried wherever I need to go in the process, polished down to my most essential self.

INVITATION FOR WRITING & REFLECTION

Do you gather or collect some natural reminder of the ways in which we are all a part of this larger, wondrous world? Write about some of the things that you collect, which ground you and bring you joy?

Pear Blossoms

They'll last for just a week or so at best,
these pear trees that have burst into wild
and riotous blossom on a neighboring street
after several nights of rain. They have opened
the doors of themselves so wide, you could
almost live inside if you were lucky enough
to be a bee, rolling around in that hidden gold,
rich and carefree for a day. But the look
of them alone is enough to make me turn back
and walk this same street twice, as if I had
nothing better to do, letting my ball cap brush
against the lowest branches so a second storm
of rainwater sprinkles down on me, and I
step like a sudden bride on white petals
strewn everywhere at my feet.

I had been feeling emotionally exhausted that spring morning, when I decided to treat myself to a walk alone.

I had been dealing with some difficult health issues with family members and had just found out that my grandmother passed away the day before. Though caught in my thoughts and sudden feelings of grief, I was stopped in my tracks when I came to a street lined with ornamental pear trees at last in bloom. Delight washed over me as I walked beneath them, smiling helplessly, a bit of rainwater dripping down on my ball cap from last night's storm. But passing through that tunnel of blossoms once just wasn't enough for me. Though I felt pulled back to phone calls with family members, I gave myself permission to circle back and walk through them once more, pausing to take a few photos and watching bees rolling around in the "hidden gold" of all that pollen. I'm struck again and again how something as simple as a short walk or brief meditation can utterly transform my mood, reminding me that, as the poet Rainer Maria Rilke once wrote, "No feeling is final." Our minds and hearts are luckily always changing and opening to the beauty of the world, even when we're grieving.

INVITATION FOR WRITING & REFLECTION

Describe a time when awe arose alongside sorrow, lifting you up, even for a brief period. How did a sense of wonder overtake the darker emotions and call you back to the world at hand? You might begin with the phrase, "As if I had nothing better to do . . ." and see where your imagination takes you.

Bluebells

Before we go inside for the night,
he insists I visit the plastic pots
which hold the Virginia bluebells
he will soon plant in the yard.
And so I do, kneeling in gravel,
examining the buds, which begin
as purple nubs, then open into blue
blossoms so bell-like I expect them
to ring as I reach out and touch
each one, with dusk coming on
and dinner yet to be made, the man
I love asking, "Aren't they beautiful?"
and me nodding to the flowers,
and the trees bursting lime-green
above us, and ferns uncurling after
a long winter sleep, each cluster
of fronds like dancers holding still
in mid-pose, my yes now including
everything alive and waking up
on this spring day like no other.

When we give our attention to the living world around us, we say a resounding yes to our own lives, and the guiding force of wonder that can lead us more deeply into presence.

This call for attention, as I describe in the poem, came for me at the insistence of my husband, who had wanted us to visit all the new plants he had bought before we went inside for the night. As I knelt there, touching a flower I'd never encountered before, some part of me blended with that living being, and this slight opening allowed me to enter the larger doorway of awareness and appreciation for all of nature. The oneness lasted for just an instant or two, but it was enough for me to carry that sensation with me back into the chores for the night—washing dishes, chopping vegetables for dinner. When we pause like this, even if we don't always want to at first, we sharpen our senses, and begin to see into things, rather than just looking at them. The Japanese poet Bashō said it best in the 17th century: "Your poetry arises by itself when you and the object have become one, when you have plunged deep enough into the object to see something like a hidden light glimmering there." This is true for all writing and creativity, and we can easily extend this truth to the art of living. In a way, our goal is to be so present in our lives that we cease to see other people and other things as objects. We become so involved with the world, so in touch with it all, that we begin to notice the hidden light—not just in bluebells and maple trees, but also in stones, wrought-iron lawn chairs, and the slats of a fence. If we intend to stay intimate with the world, we feel the same longing in everything to stay alive and thrive, from the ferns unfurling by the side of the path, to the moss on a stone wall that turns greener after each spring rain, to the trees bursting their brand-new, lime-green leaves. Each moment suddenly becomes a richer place after we take that first step, listening to the invitation to notice something outside of ourselves, and letting it change us in the process.

INVITATION FOR WRITING & REFLECTION

The next time you feel called to stray from your plans and take a break to see something more deeply, obey the invitation. Write about what you notice during this pause and try to touch on that sense of oneness.

Touch

We are changed
by the smallest gestures
of touch, as when
in my mother's final days
I smoothed the loose
gray hairs back
from her face as she
shivered all over,
smiling with pleasure.
"Like a bolt of lightning
shooting through me,"
she said, the threads
of her mind beginning
to unravel, although
I think we both knew
she was talking about love.

We don't have to be there for the exact moment when a loved one takes their final breath to know the potent awe of those final days, when each gesture or offering becomes sacred to us.

Sometimes, as was the case with my mother, we don't know until later that these are the last moments we will spend with someone. Grief then turns into a rough but nonetheless powerful blessing as we look back at those shimmering times we had together, when we did our best to let the lightning bolt of love pass between us, electric and real. I wrote a great deal after my mother passed away rather suddenly at the age of 64. She had not been well for a long time, yet all signs pointed to the possibility that she might go on as she was for months, and maybe even years. But nothing we write can ever truly hold the immensity of grief or the love we still feel for another person once they are gone. We have to release and give voice to what we feel, and yet we know over and over again that the poem or piece of writing will likely fail to capture the fullest truth of the actual moment.

Still, we can hope to re-create slivers and glimmers that honor our complex connection to the ones we have lost. Often, as in life, it is the "smallest gestures" of touch and love that stay with us the most and transport us, as well as our readers, back in time. It seems a healing miracle that, as difficult as it may feel, with just a collection of very few words, I can travel back to that hospital where I spent a week visiting my mother every day before she passed away, where I fed her, helped her take her pills each morning, and smoothed back the loose hairs from her face as she struggled with being confined to the hospital bed. Because of this poem, which arose quite suddenly for me one morning while journaling, I will never forget this slim instant that we shared, when my mother briefly became a poet as well, describing exactly how it felt to be touched by her son.

INVITATION FOR WRITING & REFLECTION

Memories of moments like this can return to us out of nowhere, especially while we are actively mourning and missing the people who once sat at the center of our lives. They surprise us with vivid detail, and often take us right back to the painful but beautiful days of a loved one's transition. Describe a similar moment of exchange, some small gesture of touch that changed you.

The Wonder of Small Things

Make much of something small—
sunlight falling on your feet
tucked beneath a fleece blanket
as you sleep in, the heat
seeping into cloth, into you.
The sound of leaves snapping off
and the slight rustle as they
settle down in their soft,
preordained places on the ground.
Purple and white asters too,
those last flowers to bloom along
the forest path, each cluster
its own constellation glowing
in the dusk that comes much
sooner now. Make much of running
a hand through the dew-tipped,
ripe seed-heads of rye grass,
or catching the flame of a single
maple leaf as it drifts, making
a wish. Open your hand and trust
whatever lands there, however
small it may seem at first.

We are used to making much of the small things that disappoint and annoy us, and which we'd desperately like to change.

Yet we are less practiced in saying yes to the small things we can almost always find, if we are looking for them, even during times of transition and upheaval. We might feel a sense of melancholy, for example, that autumn is ending, knowing the months of winter darkness and the piles of snow to come. But such thinking takes us out of the moment, which might just be filled with hidden beauties of its own. What about the rays of sun now falling across the extra fleece blanket you had to pull over you during the night? What about the purple and white asters blooming along the forest paths like constellations in the coming dusk, like the final offerings of the natural world before its long rest begins?

When we bring a playful, creative spirit to our interactions with the world, wonder tends to follow. We awaken our senses by running a hand through the dewy seed-heads of rye grass, for example, or rushing to catch a falling maple leaf, grasping that red flame like a prize in the palm. Unlocking the heart means staying open, trusting what we encounter on our path, even if it doesn't fit with our ideal, even if seems too small to be worthy of our close attention. When we choose to capture tiny instants of rapture like this in writing, we are also able to enter them again and again. French novelist Anaïs Nin once famously said, "We write to taste life twice, in the moment and in retrospect." We get to relive our moments constantly when we become very specific about what sparks our pleasure.

INVITATION FOR WRITING & REFLECTION

Make a list of the smallest, slightest things that ignite wonder and appreciation. You might begin with the line, "Make much of something small . . ." and see what images come. Follow the sensory details as they arrive without censoring or editing yourself.

The Body Electric

Every cell in our bodies contains a pore
like a door, which says when to let in
the flood of salt-ions bearing their charge,
but the power in us moves much slower
than the current that rushes into wires
to ignite the lamp by which I undress,
am told to undress by sparks that cross
the gap of a synapse to pass along
the message, *It's time for sleep.* As I pull
back the sheets, ease into bed, I think
if I could only look beneath my skin,
I'd see my body as alive as Hong Kong,
veins of night traffic crawling along
the freeways as tiny faces inside taxis
look up from the glow of their phones,
sensing that someone is watching.

As science now reveals, our bodies spark
with electricity in every moment, and
our cells develop to carry the charge of
the currents that pass through us.

These electrical signals are what allow us to think, move, and feel, constantly sending us messages—when to eat, when to sleep, when to rush out of the way of something dangerous, or move toward pleasure. I remember writing this poem not long before bed one quiet evening, thinking how much more grateful and amazed we all might feel if we could glimpse this actual electricity, and all the unseen miracles of connection, which keep our bodies functioning. To know ourselves in such an intimate, physical way might serve as a reminder to better care for this one body.

Naomi Shihab Nye has said, "Poems don't look at; they look into." Perhaps poetry is best suited for awakening the life of the spirit because it doesn't simply skirt the surface of description; instead, it also asks us to "look into," seeing more deeply into ourselves and the world than might be comfortable or customary. Every day, it seems we learn stunning new facts about humans and the living world, yet there remain so many mysteries we can't quite put into words. What is the force that animates us, that seems to watch over our bodies as they do their intricate work? Does the soul exist, and do we go on once we have left the crowded city of our body behind? We may never understand the machinery that keeps us alive for as long as possible, conducting this unseen symphony of signals, these bright freeways that conduct so much traffic through us, though we often don't feel a thing. Yet we can keep holding this one imperfect body we are given as a never-ending source of wonder.

INVITATION FOR WRITING & REFLECTION

How might your relationship to your own body change if you could glimpse even a fraction of the countless miracles that are happening just beneath the surface of awareness, even as you read this right now? Imagine yourself into the body, and see what images arise. You might also start with the phrase, "If only I could look beneath my skin . . ."

Another World

After spending all day in the house,
I stepped out toward evening
and entered another world
as soon as the sun hit my skin.
That's all it took, the light turning
like a key in the lock of me,
and the cells in my body swinging
open as I noticed bees at work
in the helianthus, every blossom
yellow-tipped, orange at the center,
like a child's drawing of the sun—
hundreds of blazing stars staring
up at me from the unnamed galaxy
of my own front yard.

We spend so much of our lives indoors, some of us in front of screens for work, that it can be easy to forget another world waits just beyond these four walls and our front door.

Once we cross that threshold, however, if we stay available and open, we will find an unnamed galaxy even in our own backyard, or in some bit of green space on the street corner. We just have to remember to look more closely, letting go of the mind's pull and the constant grind of work, to notice other lives, other worlds right in front of us. I'm fond of the quote by French surrealist poet Paul Éluard: "There is another world, but it is in this one." His words can be taken a number of ways, but most often, I think of what he said when I have been living in one world—of suffering, distraction, fear, or disappointment—and through the slightest shift in my attention, I begin to inhabit another, without having to go anywhere. Just this morning, while watering all the trees, shrubs, and perennials in our yard, I was delighted to see grasshoppers and leopard frogs leaping out of my way, as well as ants traveling the long road of the hose. I found myself stepping more softly after that, scanning each patch of grass and ground, suddenly aware of their world inside my own.

INVITATION FOR WRITING & REFLECTION

Begin with phrase, "I entered another world when . . ." and see what arises for you. You might also call forth a time in your life when you entered another world of greater mystery and wonder without having to travel very far at all.

Married to Amazement

The man I married sat next to me
after our wedding, October light pouring in
over dusty pews as he loosened his tie
and sipped from a cup of apple cider,
closing his eyes to savor the taste.

Now I think I didn't marry *him* so much
as his amazement for the everyday,
the way he still gasps each time we see
something new—baby painted turtle
plodding through a stream in the quarry,

or a neon-orange caterpillar inching
across crisp leaves on the trail,
how he kneels to film it from every angle
while I crouch beside him, in awe
of his awe, learning all that I can.

I have spent too many years living at a distance from my own body, inside my head, instead of from the energy of a more open heart.

Yet, when I met Brad, I had the feeling that I'd found someone who could teach me again the playful practice of finding wonder and awe in all things. I'll never forget our first dinner together, when he closed his eyes, tasting the hummus and tabouleh we'd ordered, savoring it until he could identify nearly every flavor, every ingredient in the recipe. That's simply how he lives his life, and I have learned a great deal just from watching him over the years. I have also carried with me Mary Oliver's famous words as a kind of mantra: "When it's over, I want to say that all my life I was a bride married to amazement, I was the bridegroom taking the world into my arms." What else is wonder but an open-armed embrace of life as it is right now?

One afternoon, as Brad and I walked the trail near our house, he spotted a bright orange caterpillar making its way across newly fallen leaves. He gasped and fell to his knees, watching its every move, then pulling out his phone to snap a few photos of its painfully slow trek across the trail. A few days later, we were walking in an old gravel quarry down the road, hoping to glimpse the great blue herons that nest in the hidden trees. Passing by one of the spring-fed streams, Brad noticed a baby painted turtle paddling along in the water. Once again, he gave a gasp and knelt on the wet, spongy ground. "I've never seen this before," he said, and it was in that moment that this poem was born.

We are drawn the most to what we need to know, and what we hope to practice in our own lives in order to grow. I believe that I was called to poetry because I have a busy and anxious mind, which knocks me repeatedly out of the present moment. I use my writing as a way of reinforcing the habit of presence and inviting myself to pause while out in the world, as my husband does quite naturally. Over the years, both my writing and my marriage have become my teachers, showing me how to reconnect with the amazement that is our birthright as humans. We do not lose the capacity for delight, but are instead trained out of the habit, taught to live by so-called logic, instead of letting our hearts guide us to the things that make us kneel and gasp with wonder for this astounding world.

INVITATION FOR WRITING & REFLECTION

Think back to a time when something made you stop and gasp. How did you pause to appreciate it, savoring the moment? See if you can re-create your own amazement with strong and specific sensory details.

GRATITUDES

This book would not exist without the inspiration and support of my readers and students, including the members of my writing community, The Monthly Pause. I thank you all for teaching me far more than I could ever teach you. This book grew out of a series of writing workshops I began to offer at Northshire Bookstore in Manchester, Vermont, and I honor the attendees who first encouraged me to use my own poems as writing prompts: Alice Gilborn, Carol Cone, Mary Ellen Rudolph, Amy Miller, Peggy Verdi, and Anna Chapman. Other inspirations and supports include: Ted Kooser, Naomi Shihab Nye, the late David Clewell, Rosemerry Wahtola Trommer, Michael Simms, Ross Gay, Elizabeth Berg, Jacqueline Suskin, Nikita Gill, Danusha Laméris, Karen Kassinger, Tara Brach, Michelle Wiegers, Erin Peacock, Michelle Stransky, and Mrs. Sharon Brown, who introduced me to the magic of poetry. Special thanks to Mark Nepo, whose teachings and books have changed my life and whose Foreword for this book is a blessing. Huge thanks to my agent, Gareth Esersky, for believing in me from the beginning, and for taking a chance on a poet. The team at Weldon Owen/Insight Editions has once again been a dream to work with; endless thanks to Katie Killebrew, Karyn Gerhard, Jon Ellis, Amanda Nelson, Roger Shaw, Raoul Goff, and everyone who helped to bring this book into the world. Lastly, I thank my husband, Brad Peacock, for encouraging me every step of the way and having endless conversations about my projects: You unlock my heart a little more every day.

ACKNOWLEDGMENTS

A number of the poems in this book have been published elsewhere, sometimes in slightly different form. I'm grateful to the editors and publishers who first gave these pieces a home:

"World Prayer Day" in *The Sun Magazine.*

"Telling My Father" in *The New Republic.*

"The Body Electric" in *The New York Times Magazine* (chosen by Naomi Shihab Nye).

"Married to Amazement" in *Rattle.*

"Fireflies" and "Night Dweller" in *The Christian Century.*

"Self-Compassion" in Academy of American Poets Poem-a-Day (edited by Kimberly Blaeser).

"Tomatoes" in *Vox Populi* (edited by Michael Simms).

"Little Altars Everywhere" and "Hermit Thrushes at Dusk" in *Cultural Daily* (edited by Bunkong Tuon).

"Evening Light," "Praise Song," and "After the Blizzard" in *Plume* (edited by Danny Lawless).

"After Burnout" and "How to Meet a Moment" in *ONE ART* (edited by Mark Danowsky).

MANDALA

An Imprint of MandalaEarth
PO Box 3088
San Rafael, CA 94912
www.MandalaEarth.com

CEO Raoul Goff
Associate Publisher Phillip Jones
Editorial Director Katie Killebrew
Senior Editor Karyn Gerhard
Editorial Assistant Jon Ellis
VP Creative Chrissy Kwasnik
Art Director Ashley Quackenbush
Senior Designer Stephanie Odeh
VP Manufacturing Alix Nicholaeff
Sr Production Manager Joshua Smith
Sr Production Manager, Subsidiary Rights Lina s Palma-Temena

MandalaEarth would also like to thank Margaret Parrish for her work
on this book.

ISBN: 979-8-88762-096-1

Manufactured in China by Insight Editions
10 9 8 7 6 5 4 3 2 1

ROOTS of PEACE   ✦ REPLANTED PAPER

Insight Editions, in association with Roots of Peace, will plant two trees for each tree used in
the manufacturing of this book. Roots of Peace is an internationally renowned humanitarian
organization dedicated to eradicating land mines worldwide and converting war-torn lands
into productive farms and wildlife habitats. Roots of Peace will plant two million fruit and
nut trees in Afghanistan and provide farmers there with the skills and support necessary for
sustainable land use.